Peaceful Selling: Easy Sales Techniques to Grow Your Small Business

Dan Duster and Stan Washington

Peaceful Selling: Easy Sales Techniques to Grow Your Small Business

Printed in the United States of America

First Printing, 2015

ISBN: 978-0-9909831-1-8

Contents

Introduction

Ever dream about having peace of mind in your business? Some business owners dread the thought of selling their product. They want sales, but they do not want to sell. They fear being viewed as the stereotypical fast-talking slickster only out for a buck. Every word out of his or her mouth reflects another pushy statement. This fear of sales causes many business owners to fail to meet their financial goal.

We've been there. Each of us has a corporate background with multi-million-dollar budget responsibilities. When we became entrepreneurs, instead of having a sales team, we *were* the team. We know how it feels to wear multiple hats. Sometimes, sales fell to the bottom of the pile. Sound familiar?

In our 30 years of corporate experience, we've seen all kinds of issues that small business owners face. Those who do not have a sales process suffer. Unfortunately, they don't understand that the sales process can be quite peaceful if done right. Yes, we really mean that!

Since we were friends from the same university, we would get together from time to time to discuss sales techniques that worked for our businesses and those that did not. We tried new methods and threw the ones away that failed. Finding the right sales methods was a journey of discovery for us.

Have you ever traveled to a different country? Often you learn more about yourself when you travel even as you learn about other cultures. That's true of sales. Finding a method that works for you and your business is the journey we're inviting you to take with us.

After hearing many questions about sales from other business owners, we developed this book to address the issues many business owners face to help you discover the same peace we found in the sales process. This book contains a custom sales process, tips, and advice for the business owner who desires to fine tune how he or she approaches new and existing customers. We'll also introduce you to the **Dual Advancement Sales Process**™ that includes advanced customer leadership to achieve higher commitment levels.

We have divided the book into three sections:

1. Preparation
   - Know Yourself
   - Prepare for the Dual Advancement Sales Process™
2. The Dual Advancement Sales Process™
   - Establish Awareness and Visibility
   - Create a Win-Win Relationship
   - Clarify Needs and Qualify Their Ability to Purchase
   - Present the Solution and Quantify the Impact
   - Gain Agreement and Make Plans
   - Close the Deal and Follow Up
3. Executing the Sales Process
   - Putting the Dual Process into Action
   - The Sales Call
   - Overcoming Objections

The Dual Advancement Sales Process™ (aka the Dual Process) can help you learn more about your prospects and customers. We cannot emphasize more the importance of asking pertinent questions to gain full understanding of a prospect's needs. In many of the chapters we will give you sample questions to start your thinking process and put you at ease during the Dual Process.

Our hope is that by the time you finish reading this book, you will feel inspired to sell, grow, and encourage others to do the same. Most of all we offer you a path toward peace.

Make every effort to keep the unity of the Spirit through the bond of peace.

Paul, also known as Saul of Tarsus, Ephesians 4:3 (NIV)

Who Is This Book For?

This book is for you if . . .

- You are a micro or small business owner selling a service or product.
- You desire to grow faster than your current pace allows.
- You sale experience fits on the continuum line between "no sales experience" and "extremely sales savvy."
- You need peace in your business.

Features of This Book

At the end of each chapter, you'll find the following sections:

Maintenance Check

The Dual Process we've provided will help your sales process run like a well-oiled machine. But even a well-oiled machine requires periodic maintenance checks. This section provides three to five tips to implement after you've considered the advice in each chapter. Choose the items that are right for you.

Relationship Check-In

At certain times throughout the book we will have you stop and review your relationship with your prospect and customers. This gives the opportunity to cement your processes and review to make adjustments to your approach if necessary.

Avoid Pitfalls

Even the simplest-to-use machine or process comes with a warning label. Our process is no different. We assembled a list of problems and pitfalls to avoid when executing the items you choose. Each section has specific warnings we collected from our experiences and from that of other experts to keep you from wasting time and money.

Section 1: Preparation

get over barriers

prepare   CRM

learn

get ready

earn

reach your goal

listen

know your product

the race is on!

lead generators

Peace or Pester—Getting Over the Barriers to Sales Success

Becoming an entrepreneur is great if it weren't for the selling, I (Stan) said to myself. My background seemed miles and miles away from "selling," or at least I thought so. I dreamt up excuses that would keep me from selling and focused on "building" more and more, rather than getting out there and drumming up business. Soon I found myself with very few customers and a nervous twitch. I then pounced on whoever was near, strong-arming them into buying my product. I wasn't at peace.

Peaceful selling really is not about being pushy; rather, it is a dual process that enables the customer to win through having a need fulfilled. You win through supplying that need.

Without steady sales, businesses starve. Your dreams of independence, supporting your family, and innovation depend on a pipeline of sales that is achievable if you can get over any barriers you have that stand in the way of your achieving those dreams. Here are a few common barriers that Dan and I and other business owners have run into over the years.

Time Management Issues

Many people are busy "doing" the work. They are so busy in fact, that they forget about creating a pipeline of sales to sustain their business. Ultimately the business fails due to a lack of time spent generating sales. I agree with making sure your product or service is sharp, crisp and well thought out. Yet at some point, taking time to find an audience becomes paramount.

Cold Calling

Cold calling is another strong fear many business owners have. They often will feel slimy and sleazy when telling people about their product. Was this due to a lack of confidence in the product? Was it the fact that they had no relationship with the prospect? I had to think about the things I felt comfortable with telling strangers and transfer those aspects into conversations where I tell people about my product.

- *Choosing what to tell strangers.* I did not mind giving a stranger driving directions, because usually they needed them and I was being helpful. I did not mind comforting a stranger when they looked sad, because I was giving them a boost up. I did not mind pointing out when a stranger was going to harm themselves by almost stepping out in traffic while they were talking on a cell phone. I had to transfer this same thinking to telling people about what my company had to offer, whether that included directions, comfort through business solutions, or timely warnings.

- *Valuing my product or service over my competitor.* Developing the solutions that we provide in Honor Services Office took four years and a ton of research. In the beginning, I was a little frightened about getting out there and selling our software. Would the software support a small business? Would it work? Was it secure enough? My confidence came from answering the questions that made me nervous. What makes you nervous about your product or service? Write down what makes you feel uncomfortable about your product or service and develop a solution.

- *Getting my timing right.* I noticed I was more susceptible to food advertisements when I was hungry. I also noticed that there were more advertisements for food right around my meal times. The largest Quick Service Restaurant (QSR) in the world places its restaurants in convenient locations so that when their advertisement plays on the radio, the consumer can quickly find the solution to hunger in minutes. Once I figured out when my customers needed our service, I could position myself to be at the right place at the right time.

Feeling Pushy

The "hard sell" seems to be the top reason why many people don't like sales. As soon as the pushy salesperson enters a party, she screams, "I'm not here to enjoy myself! I'm only here to sell!" This kind of person seems to have tunnel vision and can only see how much money can be made, rather than what solutions she can offer to meet pressing needs. The opposite of the pushy salesperson is the shy, quiet person who is quiet about his product. Instead of "selling," he can get into the habit of "telling." We will go into how to provide and present solutions later in the book.

Lack of a Goal

Many business owners purchase "open for business" signs before they set their goals for the business. They have a great product, but lack the sales goals that will help them deliver their product to the right customers. If zero is your goal, you will hit it every day. That's why setting a sales goal is vital to peaceful selling. Once you develop a goal, coming up with an adjustable plan to meet the goal becomes a lot easier.

The Fear of Building a Pipeline

Referral-only businesses are what each entrepreneur aspires to achieve. This means the product or service is so impeccable that there is no need for advertising, because customers become spokespeople for the brand. Some business owners strive to reach that goal. Many of the entrepreneurs we've met with have discovered that referrals can come too infrequently and unexpectedly. Has that been your experience?

For every sale there needs to be up to 10 prospects. In other words, once someone buys your product or service, your work is now cut out for you. You need more and more prospects in order to keep a steady flow of income.

The Marketing-as-Salesperson Mindset

People will often place ads in desperation, trying to avoid having to speak to others about the benefits of their product or service. They believe marketing and sales are one in the same. This couldn't be further than the truth. Marketing can get the attention of a prospect, but sales moves the prospect to a point of purchase.

Insecurity About a Product or Service

Failing to see the value of your product or service is one more reason why people are not confident in their offering. If you break down the benefits to yourself in the number of hours and the cost of labor, material, and overhead, you will understand why your product costs what it costs. In that way, you can feel confident that you will provide value to your customer.

The Fear of Finding Prospects

I toiled over the development of my software. When it came time to sell it, the attempt to make everyone my customer actually had the opposite effect—I had no audience. Does this sound familiar? I quickly had to set up focus groups and modify my company's offering to include what our customers were looking for. Understanding your customers and their needs, wants, and desires will be critical to the Dual Process we discuss in upcoming chapters.

Being Unprepared

When I first started out, I had one product and one service. Yet prospects kept asking about other products and services I didn't offer. They also asked me questions about my product for which I did not have answers. I had to go back to the drawing board and prepare. Preparation is extremely important to credibility, perception, and long-lasting impressions.

The Feeling of Desperation

Have you ever said or thought this: "Please oh please, buy my product!" Or, "Buy my product *now!*" Begging or being too pushy are signs of desperation. My grandmother was the best salesperson I've known. She would smile with sparkling eyes and make me think washing clothes, picking weeds, and feeding animals was a game. She sold me on doing work with her confidence, partnership attitude, and most of all, her lack of desperation for help. She could have easily done everything herself, yet sold me on working for her. You can get over the feeling of desperation by examining your source of anxiety, whether that be time, money, or other obligations.

Comparing My Company to Others

While starting out, having "startup" envy was something I had to get over. I would look at what other companies were offering and get downright discouraged. My competitors seemed well funded, well versed, and well dressed. Meanwhile I seemed to gallivant around in my horse-and-buggy of a company. Yet there is a market for "horse and buggy companies." People love them! I had to make the experience of working with my company better for my customers.

Insecurity about Success

Believe it or not, some people are not comfortable with the thought of success and all of its trappings. They have perceptions that being successful means you aren't nice, that you have to compromise your values, or that you don't deserve success. I (Dan) have had to adjust my mindset, release my limiting beliefs, and develop the confidence to be successful!

When I conduct workshops, I have participants take a vow of success and say personal affirmations. My personal affirmation is this: "The world is full of abundance. I deserve to earn what I am worth and I am entitled to be successful!" Feel free to use that or use one that is meaningful for you. What is most important is that you commit to doing well and achieving success. Developing this mindset is crucial for any entrepreneur. When you do this, you will have peace and allow prosperity to flow freely in your life.

Getting Past the Barriers

The barriers to sales success can be quite dangerous. To get past the above barriers, we are not suggesting that you become an arrogant jerk. Instead, you can add confidence, preparation, and excitement to your sales approach. Are you ready to get started on the next phase of your business?

Preparation for the Dual Advancement Sales Process™

Can you recall the last win-win situation you had? Perhaps someone told you that the service you offer enabled her business to grow. A win for both of you. That's the key to our Dual Process. We developed a step-by-step dual process, because we know stress happens to many business owners during the sales cycle, especially when they try to be someone they really aren't. They approach sales as a chore and usually don't show enough regard for the customer's true needs. Inevitably, the customer senses this and reacts negatively. As a result, that opportunity is often lost at the beginning of the sale. Does this sound familiar?

Peaceful selling helps you win at sales and eliminate unnecessary stress. It enables you to be who you are as you create a relationship of value with your customer. As you execute the elements of the Dual Advancement Sales Process™ (aka the Dual Process) you can feel confident that you and your customer are moving together towards a win-win sale. If you are too anxious to make a sale, the first tendency is to discount the product or service. The result is a loss. On the other hand, if you are too focused on the bottom line, the customer will sense you are desperate or only out to make a buck. Same result—a loss.

We can help you be successful in any sales scenario. There are four principles that build a foundation for sales success. We call these our Pillars of Sales Success. These include

- Knowledge—The introspective process of knowing your customer and your product

- Leadership—The careful process of guiding you and your customer toward a positive close
- Deliver Value—The collaborative process of providing solutions to achieve a win-win scenario
- Progress Towards Success—The measured process of taking calculated steps to achieve the dual goal.

Sales Success

| Knowledge | Leadership | Deliver Value | Progress Towards Success |

Foundational Pillars

By combining these foundational principles and utilizing the elements within the Dual Process, you will be aware of how your customer is progressing towards the sale and what adjustments you have to make to enable everyone to win and be satisfied.

Do you believe in your product or service? We hope you answered a resounding "Yes!" With the Dual Process you can bring your customer to the point of purchase and enjoy the reward of having a loyal customer who refers and returns.

Sales Success

Knowledge　Leadership　Deliver Value　Progress Towards Success

Foundational Pillars

Before you get started, have *Knowledge.*

If you know the enemy and know yourself, you need not fear the result of a hundred battles. If you know yourself but not the enemy, for every victory gained you will also suffer a defeat. If you know neither the enemy nor yourself, you will succumb in every battle.

Sun Tzu in *The Art of War*, edited by **James Clavell** (Delacorte Press, 1983)

By using this quote, we are not suggesting that your customer is your enemy or that your interactions should be considered battles. It is quite the opposite —your customer can be viewed as a partner. So, if you substitute *enemy* with *customer* and *battle* with *sales opportunity,* that quote is still accurate.

Peaceful selling requires you to have knowledge in several areas. In order to have confidence, you must know who you are as a company, who your customer is, and what their biggest challenges are. In this chapter we have listed some questions you can use to gather pertinent information that can later be leveraged to move your customer toward a successful close.

Know Your Company

People want to know who they are dealing with. They may ask, "Will you take my money and leave or will you supply superior service?" Put your customers' minds at ease and exemplify outstanding customer service while helping them understand what your company stands for.

When we studied successful salespeople, we noticed how much they knew about themselves and their company. Knowing who you are as a company gives you an edge of confidence. This involves a thorough understanding of your products and services—what they do, the problems they solve, and the impact they can have on your customer. The easiest way to probe is to ask traditional questions of the who, what, when, where, why, and how variety. Another important question to ask is, How do you determine what success is in various situations?

Questions to Consider

- Who are you? What is your brand? You can get this from your marketing approach. Your choice of marketing tactics defines your marketing approach. This is a rather large subject to cover here. If you wish to learn more, see the section on Marketing Plans in *Plans to Prosper: Strategies, systems and Tools for Small Business Marketing Success* (page 27). Knowing yourself as a brand means being consistent and standing on a communication platform that enables buy-in from your customers.

- What is a win for you? (Set SMART goals: Specific, Measurable, Attainable, Realistic, and Timely goals. You can find more on that in "Understanding the Dual Advancement Sales Process™.") For instance, instead of saying "I'm going to lose weight this year," a SMART goal would be "I'm going to lose two pounds a week for the next 10 weeks for a total weight loss of 20 pounds."

- What is the general designation for your company? Are you for profit or nonprofit?) Review your mission. Are you an entertainment company or a bus service that takes people to the entertainment? Knowing yourself may make you adjust how you service your clients. If you say you are an entertainment service, your customers will expect entertainment. But if you provide transportation to the entertainment and fail to mention the service you actually provide, your customers will complain.

- What does your company do? What problems do you solve? This is where you can shine. Who knows better than you what you do? Translating what you do so your customer can understand takes practice. Remove technical jargon, then talk to an eighth grader to practice describing what your company offers. If you can hold his or her attention as you explain what you do in layman's terms, then you have succeeded. For example instead of saying, "The multi-translator, variable-speed sustainable energy producer," why not say, "A two-gigawatt windmill that produces enough energy to run every television in your town."

- What's the startup date for your company? Credibility is formed over time. But what if you opened your doors last week? Knowing when you started shapes your message. If you are a start-up, perhaps your message will be laser focused on the benefits of your company. If you have been around awhile, perhaps your message will include how many satisfied customers you have.

- When do you provide your products/services? Customers are looking for speed, quality, or price for value. Some people don't mind waiting if the quality is high; others may want something quicker. Be ready to make adjustments if your product is seasonal or if there is high demand at certain times of the year.

- Why do you do what you do? Your customers want more than a gimmick—they want substance. What made you do what you do? Here you can express your passion for your niche of customers and appeal to their needs. If you sell to dog lovers because you love rescuing dogs, people will get excited about your purpose.

- Where are you located (city, state, region, national, international)? People are service conscious. If you have a brick-and-mortar company, your business should be in a desirable place that is easy for your customers to find. The location also informs the customer if you can relate to him or her or not. Do you really know about snow chains if you live in sunny Florida? Credibility is sometimes established by location.

- How do you do what you do? ? How do you deliver? Customers need to know how you make your product so they can feel great about buying your product or service. For example, quality hand-stitched dresses or premium wood lathes that cut through hardwood. Do you deliver overnight? Just how impressive will you be for your customer?

You can also communicate who you are in a succinct message that can be articulated in less than a minute. This is what is commonly known as *your 30 second spiel*. You should develop and practice your spiel so that you can say it with accuracy and confidence to anyone, anytime.

Knowing your products also means knowing the impact they have on your customer. This will make you *FABulous* to your customer. What is *FABulous?* Know the *Features* of your products, the *Advantage* that it creates, and the *Benefit* to your customer. For example, "This car is aerodynamic (Feature); it gets better gas mileage (Advantage), which means you will save money (Benefit)."

If your company has developed a marketing plan, you can draw from the elevator pitch you put together in your marketing approach to get the features, advantages, and benefits. An elevator pitch is a short statement (around 40 words or so) about your business. It should typically include who you are, what you do, how long you've been doing it, what impact you've had, and why you are effective. Dan's elevator pitch is 43 words: "I'm a motivator and success coach. For over 15 years, I've helped thousands of people achieve and enjoy their wildest dreams by establishing their vivid vision for success, getting them to believe they deserve it and creating a plan to do it."

Stan's elevator pitch for Honor Services Office is 35 words: "We help businesses grow immediately and effectively through our business management software. We serve women, veterans and underserved small businesses through custom sales, marketing, and technology workshops enabling confidence in the professionalism of their business."

You also need to know your limitations. What is the maximum amount of work you can take on? What are the limitations of your products/services? You don't necessarily need to tell people this, but it is definitely important for you to know so that you take on the right clients and deliver what you promise.

Know Your Customer

"So, do you want to buy my widget?" a salesperson belched out at the customer. "No thanks," the customer replied. This shallow conversation was repeated over and over without any business transactions resulting. Instead of a pushy statement that a customer would walk away from, the conversation could have gone like this:

Salesperson: Hi Jan, how is your implementation project going? I hope it's going well.

Customer: It's having its challenges, but we're getting through it.

Salesperson: Remember how long it took for the last implementation? I will help you with a solution that works within your budget.

Customer: Great!

Knowing your customer's language is vital to helping them understand how your solution fits their need.

Questions to Consider

- Who
    - Who is your prospect?
    - What is her title, position, and/or department?
    - What are his responsibilities?

- o   Who reports to him?
- o   To whom does she report?

Knowing *who* your customer is and what she does will naturally allow you to better address her needs. If you have analyzed your market, you will understand your customer and his or her ability to purchase.

- What
    - o   What do they need?
    - o   What products do they want?
    - o   What do they currently have?
    - o   What are their deliverables?
    - o   What are their challenges?
    - o   What is their budget?

By asking *what* questions, you can determine tangible concrete solutions within a defined scope.

- When
    - o   When are they prepared to make a purchase?
    - o   When will you get approval or payment?

When questions determine the portion of your service level agreement and how quickly you will react to the sale, problem/resolution, or inquiry.

- Where
    - o   Where is your customer located?
    - o   Where does your customer serve?

As mentioned above in "Know Your Company," understanding location means you understand its challenges. Some examples of geographical challenges determined from *where* questions might include: delivery barriers, weather-related corrosion, and cultural aspects.

- Why
    - o   Why is your prospect looking to make a change?
    - o   Why are they looking at your product?

Understanding *why* may help you understand the thought, emotion, or spirit behind the purchase. Purchasing a cake is one thing, but if a customer is purchasing a birthday cake, the purpose has been established. Through more probing to understand why, you may find out this is a "special" birthday. Therefore, add-ons can be discussed.

- How
    - How are decisions made?
    - How are things approved?

How questions help you determine the interest level, understand the customers' engagement level, and understand their decision process so you can adjust your goals and approach.

Research Your Customer

In the book *Plans to Prosper: Strategies, Systems and Tools for Small Business Marketing Success,* there is a section that clearly lays out how to research your market by doing a market survey. Here are a few things to do to understand how to research your customer:

- Do an online search for the company to identify specific problems for which you can provide solutions.
- Go to the library and leverage the business section or a local business center to understand your customer more.
- Read newsletters about the group you are dealing with. For example read publications that help prepare stay-at-home moms for transition back into the workforce.

Know Success

If someone were to say, "I want a bottle of water," how would you know what he really wants? What would success look like? Well, after staggering out of a burning desert, the simple task of drinking water is a great success. However, in an office environment, a bottle of water can range from an eight-ounce bottle to a one-gallon jug or a five-gallon replacement for the water cooler. So the definition of success in that instance can vary greatly. Knowing success in sales means that you have an understanding of the needs and expectations of the customer and know how those align with reaching your own goals.

Knowing your customer's definition of success also is key. What are her expectations of your product/service? You can ask her directly: "If this is implemented correctly, how will you know it is successful? What will success look like?" If you don't know your customers' expectations, chances are you won't be able to meet them. You must know what they really want to happen so that you are sure you can provide a solution that will satisfy their needs.

You also need to know the answers to the following questions:

- What does success look like for you?
- What are you trying to accomplish in this situation?
- At what price, cost or investment is it worth it for you to do this particular deal?

Know when a deal is not worth your time or resources and be comfortable with avoiding a less-than-worthwhile opportunity. As the chorus of the well-known Kenny Rogers song, "The Gambler," remind us, you have to know when to fold and walk away.

Know Your Competition

We watched a restaurant open and risk closing within six months. It wasn't because their food was bad; it was actually quite delicious. At lunch the other eateries were full and this one was lacking. The restaurant owners went to the other restaurants in the area and soon found out that one competitor was baking fresh bread and giving some away to take home and another competitor gave samples of upcoming meals while their patrons chowed down on the special of the day. "We have to come up with a plan" they said after visiting their competition.

Questions to Consider

- Do you have to know the major competitors in your market?

Knowing your competitors helps you understand what product or services you should be offering. It also helps you determine what price to establish for your product or service.

- What do they provide?

Study your competitors' product mix, the words they use to describe their product, and any extra services they are giving away as part of their offering.

- What are their strengths and weaknesses?

Understanding your competitors' strengths and weaknesses helps you craft your message to address any deficiencies your product may have, while keeping in mind a positive spin of the advantages.

- Why you are different and how does that difference make you a better fit for potential customers?

Different is sometimes viewed as bad to some, so it will be up to you to tell potential customers why they would be better off using your product or service. Your product will need to be five times better to make your customer switch.

- How does your price compare to theirs and how do you justify what your price point?

Pricing is extremely important. If you desire to be on the high end, then have a superior product than all of your competitors. Remember, your customer may define *value* differently than you.

Putting the Knowledge Together

By knowing your company, product, service, market, customer, buying trends, and decision makers, you can feel at peace, knowing that you have enough information to develop solid solutions for your customer.

Maintenance Check

- Make an effort to gain a thorough knowledge in the key areas mentioned above. Keep this information in a Customer Relationship Management (CRM) tool like Honor Services Office.

- Practice your 30-second spiel before different audiences. You can practice with a child to make sure that your message is captivating, yet simple. Practicing with adults shows that you know your company and can articulate your mission statement succinctly and with confidence.

- Write several FABulous statements.

Avoid Pitfalls

- The biggest pitfall to avoid is trying to be someone you are not. Remain yourself and you will do fine.

- Another pitfall involves taking on customers whom you suspect will not be good customers. Use your gut and carefully assess the information you gleaned.

- One pitfall we often fall into is taking on more than we can handle. Understand your company's capacity, your customer's budget, and your own bandwidth to deliver an excellent product or service.

Before you get started, have *Sales Leadership.*

If you build it, he will come.

Field of Dreams (1989; screenplay by Phil Alden Robinson)

Many entrepreneurs and salespeople think that if they have nice product, people will buy it. "If I build it, they will come." That could happen, but a sale is not guaranteed. So, how do you get people to their destination—to go from Point A to Point B? You have to lead them there!

One of the simplest ways to think of leadership as it relates to sales is being able to "lead the ship." Imagine you are a captain of a tour boat. You need to treat your customers like you plan a vacation.

One of the vacations that comes to mind is an exotic getaway I (Stan) took with my family. We got excited about the place we chose and the stops along the way. We fully understood the costs, and as an added bonus, we received information on some deals to include. We had the time of our lives.

Making a sale is very similar to being a tour guide. With that in mind, here are some tips to guide you in this venture.

Know the sales destination.

Think of the sales destination as the knowledge of how your product or services can impact a client's business or life. First, you need to know what your customer wants and needs. Second, you need to discern how your product or service solves those needs. The way to do this is to ask questions to find out what your client needs. But you have to keep probing to get at what a client really wants.

Let's take this pretend vacation conversation as an example:

Travel agent: Where do you want to go on vacation?

Client: Jamaica.

Travel agent: Why Jamaica?

Client: I like the beach.

Travel agent: I know a great beach in Jamaica.

So, the travel agent books the client on a vacation at a beach in Jamaica. The beach has water sports, bars, and lots of activities. Yet it turns out the client likes the beach for quiet and relaxation. He does not like the chosen vacation spot! The travel agent did not take the time to get to know the client's needs.

In the same way, you've got to know your prospect's destination and why they want to go in order to deliver the correct solution!

Be a flexible sales process tour guide.

It is up to you to guide the process. Each customer and situation is different. You have to respond to each customer on an individual basis. Be flexible with how you interact with a customer and how you want the sales process to flow. You can't expect the same sales spiel to work for every customer. For example, my father wanted a mobile phone. He was a very simple man with modest needs. He only made a few calls a month, so he just wanted a simple phone— no smartphone, no data package, no text package, just something to let him make phone calls. I (Dan) took him to the store and watched the salesperson lose the sale.

He kept trying to get my father to purchase a smartphone by saying how useful it would be with all of the features it had. My father insisted that he only needed a flip phone. The salesman told him that with a smartphone, my father could listen to music, surf the internet, get sports scores, and several other things. My father finally got frustrated, and we left. That salesperson lost the sale because he wasn't flexible and wouldn't adjust his sales pitch to what the customer wanted.

We went to another store. This time the salesperson asked my father what he wanted and how he intended to use the phone. He listened attentively, then showed my father three choices of phones and offered the simplest package they had. My father got the phone he wanted and the salesperson earned a sale and a satisfied customer. This just shows that you have to listen to your customer and be flexible in providing a solution to them.

Highlight relevant benefits or attractions and check in along the way.

Your customers are your "passengers." Make sure they are engaged in the sales journey and they are "on board" with where you are going. You have to be able to highlight things that are important to them and check in to make sure that you are addressing their desires or concerns. If you lose passengers along the way (at least mentally), there won't be anybody with you when you get to your destination. That means you can go in the direction *you* want, but the customer ultimately won't buy.

I have been on several tours in Chicago. One was a black history tour for my family reunion. The guide started by giving us a lot of information about different black-owned restaurants and where some famous people lived. About a third of the way into the tour, she asked us how it was going. I was candid and said that we were more interested about the evolution and economic development of certain neighborhoods. She thanked me and highlighted much more of those things for the rest of the tour. The family loved it and I've recommended that tour to several people since then.

In sales, you need to know what benefits might be important to the customer so that you can highlight what is relevant to them and keep them engaged in the sales process. Also, checking in occasionally is helpful to make sure that you are catering to their desires.

Cater to the whole team.

Check to see that the right people are involved in the process. If you are dealing with more than one person, find out who the decision maker is, who the influencers are, and how you can keep them involved in the process. You must continually gain agreement from each of them that you are solving their problems and headed to a destination they will be happy with.

Consider how the destination of a family vacation is chosen. In some cases, the husband may pay for it, but he is not necessarily the decision maker. The wife and kids need to be happy with the destination!

When I was a sales rep for Abbott, I was selling an instrument involved in chemistry tests for a hospital lab. The general tendency is to sell to the lab manager and to the purchasing department, because the manager is the decision maker and ultimately the purchasing department has to approve it. I decided to involve the pathologist also, because he would benefit by having more accurate test results. I talked with the lab techs also, because they would benefit from using an instrument that would make their jobs easier and save them a lot of hassle. I was able to win out over the competition, because all of the stakeholders knew how my solution would help them directly.

Make sure you have a quality crew and ample supplies.

This means making sure you have the right resources to deliver your solution on time. The right resources include having the right people from your team involved with the process. When I worked at IBM as a sales rep, I was part of a team of people who sold computers to financial service firms. One time, I made a commitment to a customer, saying that we would be able to install a complex computer system in two to four weeks (our standard length of time). After checking with my team to see who would be responsible for doing the installation, they told me there was no way for the installation to take place.

One person was taking a vacation and one of the memory devices took four to six weeks to order; they would need some additional memory as well. So, I had to go back to the customer and explain to him that the solution was going to take longer and cost more than anticipated. Needless to say, he wasn't pleased, but he still made the purchase.

The bottom line is, if your solution needs other people (your crew) to make it happen, you need to check with them to make sure you can commit to doing it. There is nothing worse than gaining agreement on a solution (product or service) and then not being able to deliver it to the customer. Disappointment after a decision is made is worse than saying up front that an option wasn't available in the first place.

Obtain buy-in.

Once you have presented the solution, close the sale and make the customer feel good about it. We have seen so many salespeople get the prospect to agree to everything, but they don't ask them to buy. You must ask for the deal, get them to buy, *and then* make sure they are happy about it.

Relationship Check-In

- Know what the customer wants or needs.
- Guide the process instead of following your customer's alternate process.
- Ask questions to make sure you highlight what your customer wants or needs.
- Seek out and involve the right people (on both sides).
- Close the deal by asking for your potential customer's business.

Avoid Pitfalls

- Try not to make assumptions about what the customer wants. Ask questions to clarify their vision of success.
- Don't promise anything you can't deliver.

Before you get started, know how to *Deliver Value.*

When you show people that you have a solution that is specific to their needs, you deliver value. When you deliver value to a person, you can have a customer for life!

One time on vacation, I (Stan) stopped at a quaint souvenir shop and happened to see a salesperson speaking with the general manager of the store. He was raving to him about a plastic substitute product that could bring in higher profits. The reluctant GM said, "We aren't trying to sell junk to make money." I believe those were the only words from the GM.

As the salesperson went on and on about the benefits, I could see the body posture of the GM tense up. The sale was clearly lost. After the salesperson left, I asked the GM about his product. I could see his face light up as he was the one who carefully made his trinkets by hand. He told me he would like to sell more, but it took time to handcraft everything.

I asked him if he made the gum and bottled water he sold over the counter. He laughed and said he knew where I was going. I then said to him, "I wonder if you could add a product that showcases your craftsmanship and supports your values." He asked me to tell him more.

The salesperson couldn't make the sale, because he didn't know the most important component of selling. He didn't know how to deliver value. He didn't know what was important to the customer or how to provide a solution that would meet his needs.

Value to the Customer

First, you must deliver value to your customer. This is the person, company, or group to whom you are selling. Value = Experience + Quality/Price. Value doesn't always mean profit, but it helps steer you in that direction. The customer has a reputation to uphold. They must feel confident that your product or service upholds their reputation. And as mentioned in the statement at the top of the page, when you show a customer you are helping them, they will see your value and will remain loyal for life!

The second part of delivering value to the customer should include delivering value to the customers they serve. This person buys from your customer and is the reason why your customer is in business. Meeting with your stakeholder to understand their customer is important to do on a regular basis. Look for why the customer would buy the product.

Value to Your Company

Ultimately, your company needs to have sales that are profitable in order for your company to be profitable. To make that profit, your price may seem high to your customer or even higher than some of your competitors. So, you need to understand your value so that you can justify your pricing. Is your product or service sold at a higher price point because it is rare or the materials are expensive? Do you have extra services that come with the product you are selling? Whatever the case may be, you should be able to justify the pricing in order to make reasonable profits.

When I (Dan) worked for Abbott Diagnostics, we had discounted pricing for high-volume customers. I had a proposal for a hospital that listed our standard pricing. The chairman of the review committee happened to work for another hospital that received the discounted pricing and he inquired (suspiciously) as to why this hospital would be paying more. I explained our policy and they agreed, *and* bought the product!

Long Term versus Short Term

Sometimes you may have to do things that only allow you to break even or perhaps suffer a loss at the time. You need to consider how valuable a transaction may be in order to have long-term benefits. This can include a trial offer with a reduced price, breaking even to get referrals or testimonials, or other creative ideas to help you gain business.

I (Dan) have a friend who published a great motivational book. She received an offer from an organization that wanted to buy over 5,000 copies. She said that they couldn't come to an agreed-upon price, so she never made that sale. My thought is that if she could have broken even, she would go onto the bestseller list automatically. You can't buy that type of opportunity to have great publicity.

Maintenance Check

- Ensure that your product solves your customer's problem (delivers value).
- Review your pricing policy (know your value).
- Make an effort to deliver value to the customer and your company.
- Research your competitors' products and price mix. Determine the value each competitor offers.

Avoid Pitfalls

- Be aware of your competitors' pricing. Just because theirs is low doesn't mean yours has to be. Value is key so make sure your pricing includes quality service.
- Do not be fooled into the belief that value is only price based.
- Don't be so eager to have the lowest price in order to gain more business. You may get a higher quality customer who is willing to pay a premium price if your services warrant it.
- Don't focus only on the current situation to determine if something is worth doing. Sometimes you may need to go with a deal you aren't thrilled about right now in order to cultivate a larger opportunity in the future.

Before you get started, know how to *Progress toward Success.*

Do not confuse motion and progress. A rocking horse keeps moving but does not make any progress.

Alfred A. Montapert, *The Supreme Philosophy of Man: The Laws of Life* (Prentice-Hall, 1977)

Have you ever had one of those moments where at the end of the day you know you were busy all day, but you really can't tell that you were productive? Often times we may do things that occupy our time, but they don't produce meaningful results. For example, in preparing for a marathon, you can spend time choosing which shoes to wear, lacing your shoes perfectly, making sure your clothes are color coordinated, ironing your outfit, or you can choose to run. The rest of those activities will keep you busy, but running is what will allow you to progress toward success.

It is most important to remember that all of your efforts and actions should be geared toward moving the process forward and making the customer successful. Sales is similar to a marathon. Marathon race preparation has been used over and over to get a point across, mainly because a marathon is extremely hard to run. Many try and fail and the grueling preparation is not desirable, but those who reach the finish line have a great sense of accomplishment.

The same is true with sales. While some deals close right away, others may feel like a marathon, because they take seven times longer than others. Though you might be tempted to do so, make sure you don't quit in the middle of the race. Instead, continue to advance the process even if your potential customer takes longer to buy than you would like him or her to do.

Purposeful Meetings

Meeting preparation is covered more thoroughly in the chapter about that, but there are a few things to keep in mind no matter what. Each meeting you have with a customer should be designed to advance the sales process. You need to have an agenda with your optimal goals clearly thought out, as well as the minimum goals you want to accomplish in that meeting.

You should not "meet to meet" or "just to stop by." When I (Dan) worked for other companies, I had several meetings where we didn't have a specified purpose just to show to my manager that I had activity in these accounts.. Sometimes at these meetings we did not talk about business at all. I was *active*, but I was not *advancing* the sale. As an entrepreneur, I don't have that luxury. I have to close business or I don't eat. Perhaps that's true of you. That's why I implore you to meet with a purpose. Having goals for your meeting time shows respect for your customer and most importantly, respect for yourself and your time. Here are some suggestions for meeting with purpose:

- Have a formal or informal agenda prepared at all times.
- Look for problems, issues, and metrics that will enable you to get to know your customer better and enable you to service him more effectively.
- Assess what's going on at the given location. What are the employees doing? What are the demographics?

Establishing and Enhancing the Relationship

Meeting people builds a strong pipeline. I have seen people fail miserably at this, because they go into the relationship thinking about sales. Progression in the relationship means understanding the needs of your customer. The initial meeting is all about them and their needs.

Leverage a CRM Tool like Honor Services Office to document notes on all of your meetings. You will leverage these notes to further understand the problems the buyer is facing and build a strategy to solve those problems.

When you look for ways to enhance your relationship with your customer, you gain loyalty. Find out enough about them so that you can create ways to have meaningful interaction with them. Ask about their interests and their challenges. Tell them you want to deliver value and ask them how you can most effectively share information with them. When you see an article or resource that can help them, forward that information to them. This positions you as a partner and provider of solutions which creates a value-based relationship that distinguishes yourself from your competition.

Prioritize Your Customer's Problem

Your customer might not be able to prioritize their problems, because they are too close to the issues. This is where you come in. Helping them make sense of their issues enables better conversations and will foster a spirit of collaboration. Get them out of firefight mode and onto a process of solution development. Here are some suggestions:

- Let your customer list as many problems as they can mention.

- Help them prioritize the problems to address the ones with the highest impact.

- Gain agreement about which ones are most important and why. (Try to narrow the list.) This will help you tailor your solution to address their key concerns.

You'll find out more about prioritizing in section 3 of the sales process.

Be Solution Driven

So many salespeople focus on trying to get the customer to buy instead of providing a solution to their problems. When you focus on providing a solution, several positive outcomes can result. For example:

- Reinforce your relationship with your customer as being value based.

- Expand your thinking to address the problem to develop a bigger solution (and sale) than your customer may have initially thought about.

- Partner with other vendors to deliver that solution. This could drive additional sales through those partnerships.

Follow Up

"Thank you" is rarely heard, but is an obligation if you want to have long-term success in sales. Thanking a person for her valuable time strengthens the relationship and keeps your name in front of your customer. You must follow up with any obligations you promised during your meeting. This is important to do even if it means updating your customer to report that you haven't finished a task, but are working on it. If you do not express a sense of urgency, your customer will drop away quickly.

- Follow up within 24 hours. You might thank your customer with a phone call or email.

- Send a note through the mail if you can. This is rarely done these days and will make you stand out. Be brief in your thank you note, but state something meaningful from the conversation. For example: "Thank you for explaining your warehouse upgrade program. It sounds exciting."

 **Maintenance Check**

- Keep advancing the sales process uppermost in your mind.

- Consider solving the customer's problems with your products or services in a customized way.

- Keep in mind that creating a value-based relationship is better than a sale, because referrals also can come from customers who say no as well.

⚠ Avoid Pitfalls

- Steer clear of the thought that being busy is the same as forward progress. When you see *fill out the vendor paperwork* on the website, realize that this process is a hurdle placed in front of you. You can become very busy and remain in a holding pattern. Fill out the paperwork, and then ask what needs to happen next.

- Don't give up too soon. Sometimes it takes more than seven contacts with your prospect before you land the deal.

- Be careful of "just meeting to meet." Have a purpose for everything you do to avoid wasting words.

Section 2: The Dual Advancement Sales Process™

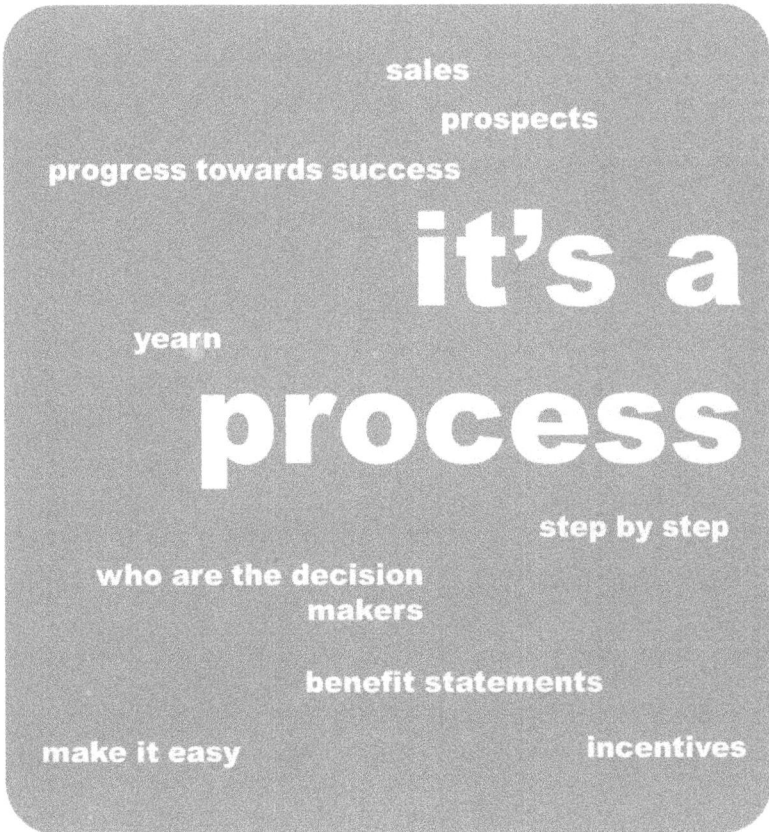

sales

prospects

progress towards success

it's a

yearn

process

step by step

who are the decision makers

benefit statements

make it easy   incentives

Dual Advancement Sales Process™

Overview of the Dual Process

Customer Mindset	**Consultative Sales Step**
Not Interested	Establish Awareness and Viability
Some Interest	Create a Win-Win Relationship
Very Interested	Clarify Needs and Qualify Their Ability to Purchase
See Value	Present Solution and Quantify
Convinced	Gain Agreement and Make Plans
Committed	Close Deal and Follow Up

Understanding the Dual Advancement Sales Process™

A successful sales process really does not look like selling. It is quite natural and there are distinct steps to the process that if missed, can cause a higher chance of a lost sale. The Dual Advancement Sales Process™, also known as the Dual Process, is unique in that it helps you advance yourself and the customer through stages, ultimately reaching a successful sale. It has two parts: the *Customer Mindset* and the *Consultative Sales Steps,* also known as techniques. See figure 1 below.

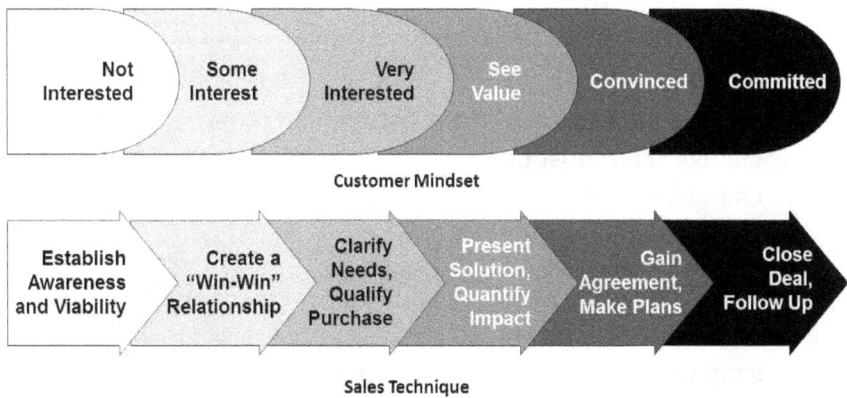

| Not Interested | Some Interest | Very Interested | See Value | Convinced | Committed |

Customer Mindset

| Establish Awareness and Viability | Create a "Win-Win" Relationship | Clarify Needs, Qualify Purchase | Present Solution, Quantify Impact | Gain Agreement, Make Plans | Close Deal, Follow Up |

Sales Technique

Figure 1—Dual Advancement Sales Process™

We designed the Dual Process because most sales processes are one sided. They tend to heavily focus on the customer, while leaving out the company's goals. This precipitates a win-lose situation. Another sales process which focuses on the company's goals leads to a too-aggressive sales team, customers feeling badgered into buying, and numerous complaints from disgruntled customers. The primary goal of the Dual Process is to create a lasting win-win relationship that breeds add-on, repeat, and referral purchases.

There is an art to assessing where your customer is and where you are in the sales process. We're confident you can do this consistently once you have learned all of the steps.

To land the deal, you have to bring a customer from Not Interested to Committed. Depending on the type of product, price, and availability, this can happen over time or within one conversation. As you have conversations with your prospects and customers, the trust level goes up and they are willing to give more information to gain what they really want. They go from shallow answers to deeper, meaningful needs, and ultimately full disclosure.

Here are some rules about the Dual Advancement Sales Process™:

1. You cannot move faster than your customer. In other words, if you are ready to close and they are at the Very Interested stage, you will not close.

2. You can go through all of the stages of the sales process in one conversation or one year. All steps hold true, regardless of time.

3. You may have to backtrack between steps as commitments change. You must be aware of how quickly the climate may change, which may cause you to leverage techniques from a previous step in the sales process.

By understanding where you are and where you customer is in the sales process, you will be able to address specific issues that may arise during that phase. Sit back and review the sales process over the next few chapters.

Set Your Sales Goal

Be S.M.A.R.T. about setting your sales goal. In other words, be . . .

Specific. Have specific sales numbers you would like to reach.

Measurable. Know what success looks like in measurable quantities.

Attainable. Work within the resources of your company and your customers' constraints.

Realistic. Avoid under promising and over delivering. Never set unrealistic deadlines, deals, or discounts.

Timely. Have the right solution at the right time and provide it to your customer expeditiously.

An example of a SMART sales goal would be: I am going to sell 10,000 copies of my book by September 30.

When setting goals, I (Stan) try to understand the entire picture. I leverage information available to me to determine the likelihood of a sale. This means I have to prepare before I set goals.

Preparation for Sales Goals

Understanding my prospects is where I begin. Knowing the number of prospects, their names, contact information, and needs helps me remain focused. I can then project how many will purchase within a given period of time based on sales history.

First, I review how long it took to land previous sales to determine if the "time to close" is realistic. Being able to close a sale in just one meeting would be ideal, but the higher the price, the longer the sales cycle. Second, I review whether I can reach the number of people I need to reach in order to meet my sales goal. Third, I review the timeline for my goal. I leave enough room so I don't get into a panic. No one likes a panicked salesperson.

Preparation gives me peace. For example: We will sell 10% more of our homemade apple juice to the community five miles west of our office next month.

Maintenance Check

- Remember to be realistic with your sales goals. We all want to sell a million in one day; check to make sure this is attainable.
- Keep in mind that the Dual Advancement Sales Process™ can be iterative. One sale is not like the next. You may have to repeat certain stages until you advance to the next stage.

Avoid Pitfalls

Avoid throwing in the towel on your first mistake. Being effective at sales takes practice and mistakes may happen. Learn from them and improve your approach.

Dual Advancement Sales Process™

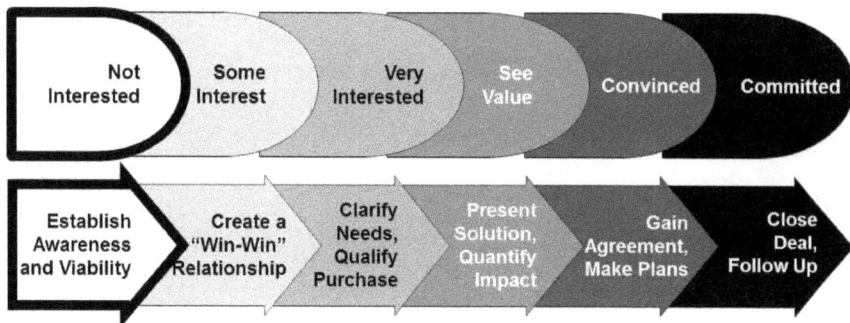

Not Interested	Some Interest	Very Interested	See Value	Convinced	Committed
Establish Awareness and Viability	Create a "Win-Win" Relationship	Clarify Needs, Qualify Purchase	Present Solution, Quantify Impact	Gain Agreement, Make Plans	Close Deal, Follow Up

Dual Process Step 1: Establish Awareness and Viability

Years ago, a friend of mine (Dan) asked me to go car shopping with her so she could have a male's opinion. Upon arriving at the dealership, the salesman assumed that I was the buyer and focused all of his attention on me. He didn't ask her any questions; he just talked to me and listed feature after feature that she really didn't care about. After five minutes of hearing him talk, she cut him off, told him that she was the one interested, and that he lost a sale. We left the dealership. He lost the sale, because he assumed when he should have assessed. It is better to assess than to assume.

Customer Mindset: Not Interested

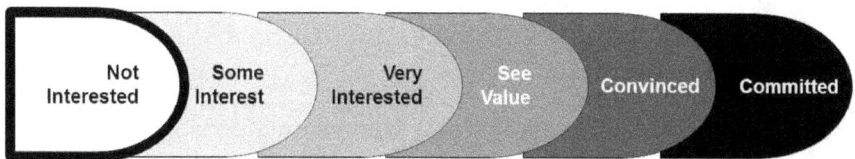

| Not Interested | Some Interest | Very Interested | See Value | Convinced | Committed |

This potential customer doesn't know who you are or what services you provide. Let them know enough about what you do in order to gain their interest and learn how you can help them. At the same time, you want to find out enough about her to make sure that she is the correct target. Also, you want to know if she is the decision maker. If not her, who is?

Recognize *Not Interested Open* versus *Not Interested Closed*

Not Interested is a state in which your prospect is unaware that your product or service exists. His mind could be focused on making a purchase of another type and it is up to you to bring awareness to him. A prospect can be deemed *Not Interested but Open* or *Not Interested but Closed*. An "Open" person may not be interested yet whereas the "Closed" person is not likely to be interested at all. Here are some tips for discerning the mindset of prospects:

Browsing. Recognize when your prospect is actually in search of products or services like yours. They may volunteer information like, "I'm in the market for something that fixes my widget (whatever business problem is relevant for your customer)." Asking the right questions regarding her search will be key to moving a browser into the Dual Process. This prospect is savvy and has researched products or services. Communicate to (otherwise known as *touch*) this person at least three times within a six-week period.

Unaware. Prospects who are unaware may or may not be in the market for your product or any other. The information you present may be the first time they heard of a product or service like yours. Make a lasting impression by asking general questions about them and keep in contact with them. Communicate to this person once every six weeks.

Closed. It is usually very obvious when someone is not at all interested in your company. Handling this person right, however, can win him or her over to your product or service. I (Stan) met a salesperson who was so impressive with his knowledge I had to stop and listen. He was extremely personable and passionate. I took his card and when I was in the market for his service, I looked him up. This made me realize that instead of thinking that a prospect is closed forever, I could say, "He's closed for now."

Consultative Sales Step: Establish Awareness and Viability

This is the beginning of your peaceful journey. The purpose of this step is to help your customer gain an awareness of you, your company, and what you have to offer. Sometimes this awareness will move the person to the point of purchase quickly, because they may have a need, but have not started looking for a solution.

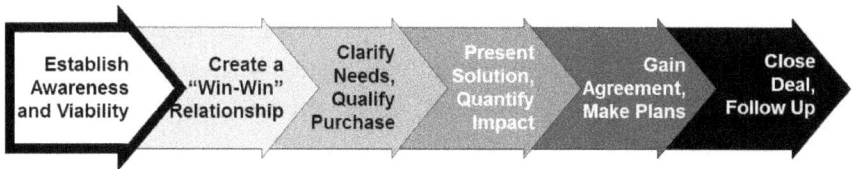

Gather Information

This is the point in your journey where you get to know your prospect or their company and decides if it is worth pursuing their business.

- **Prospecting.** You should know the proper contacts and they should be aware of you and the services you provide. You and the customer should be able to decide if your business relationship is worth moving to the next step based on the knowledge that you have shared.

- **Benefits Statement.** Capture the customer's interest and earn the right to move forward.

- **Gather Vital Information.** Ask enough questions to gain a general understanding of who that person is and what role they have within their company.

Gather Customer Information. Collect as much contact information as possible to enter into your CRM. Take vital notes on each meeting leveraging the who, what, when where, why and how questions. (For more about these questions, see "Before you get started, have *Knowledge.*")

Gather Competitor Information Specific to This Customer. If your customer has a brick-and-mortar business, drive a two-mile radius and document their competitors' prices, services, and offerings. Leverage this information when developing your solution. If your customer has a home-based or virtual business, research them online, starting in their geographic area to cut down on noisy searches.

Prospect List. Add each potential client or prospect to a CRM tool like Honor Services Office. Separate the contacts by industry, geography, or other specific grouping so you can do a mass communication to these individuals to save time, as well as keeping your prospects moving towards "Some Interest."

The Goal of the First Meeting

When I (Stan) prepare for a sales meeting, I look at it as more of an opportunity to serve, rather than to sell. This means I need to find out as much information about the customer as possible in order for me to provide the best service.

When first meeting someone, the same principles apply whether you are selling to them or deciding if you should date. By getting to know them a little and what they are interested in, you will be on your way to developing a long-lasting relationship. From there, you decide, "Should we do business?"; "Should we develop solutions together?" "Are we in the same ballpark in terms of expectations?" "Is there enough interest to move forward?"

People often make this step too complicated or start selling too quickly before they have asked enough questions. It is important for you to show interest in your prospect and his or her business. Make an effort to understand him or her before you start selling. Ask questions, listen attentively. The prospect should be doing most of the talking. The ultimate goal of this meeting is to collect as much information about the customer as possible.

Use Active Engagement

Active engagement is a conversation that flows freely instead of being forced. Here, you can remain focused on what your customer is saying, rather than thinking of what you will say next. Since you may not know what the problem is, you may have to carefully probe by using follow-on questions.

Mirror their questions and responses. By using the mirror technique, you gain clarity in the conversation. Your customer will appreciate if you clarify questions she may have asked or reflect back statements she uttered. For example when your customer says, "We are having a problem with collaborating" you could mirror and clarify by saying, "Let me see if I have this straight. You and your team are having a problem collaborating. Is that correct?" Now that you have mirrored, ask a clarifying question: "What does successful collaboration look like to you?"

Use a Survey

Your first meeting can be strictly an information gathering meeting. By asking people to participate in a focus group, you can survey their opinions, needs, and wants. Please be cognizant of your prospects' time. The longer the survey, the more you may have to compensate them.

Some surveys ask:
- How likely are you to purchase within the next 30 days?
- What product or service do you use now? How satisfied are you?
- How many times a year do you purchase this product or service?

Whatever information you wish to collect, mix the questionnaire with open-ended questions, multiple choice, and questions with "yes" or "no" answers.

Let's revisit Dan's dealership conversation. Here is how the conversation could have gone if the salesperson took time to ask questions.

Dealer: Hello. Thanks for coming to this car dealership. How can I help you?

Buyer Consultant: We're just looking at some cars.

Dealer: Oh that's fine. Are you looking for a car together, or is it for one of you in particular? *(Be sincerely interested.)*

Buyer Consultant: It is for Sarah. *(Motions to Sarah.)*

Dealer: Okay, Sarah, what are you looking for in a car? *(Be curious.)*

Buyer: I need a car that looks pretty nice and gets good gas mileage.

Dealer: What do you do with your time? What are the major things you are going use the car for?

Buyer: I'm a marketing rep, so I have to travel to client locations a lot. Sometimes I will take them to lunch in my car. So, I also need something that has a smooth ride.

Dealer: Okay. So what is your price range?

Buyer: I'd like to pay no more than $400 a month.

Dealer: Good deal. So, if I can show you a car that looks nice, gets good gas mileage, has a smooth ride and comes in under $400 a month, would that make you happy?

Buyer: Yes! *(Seems invested now.)*

Dealer: Great! Let's look at _____ .

In this example, you can see how the dealer didn't make any assumptions about the customer. He was able to assess the situation by asking questions and fully listening to what the customer wanted.

Relationship Check-In

- See how the dealer in this example speaks directly to the customer, uses probing questions, and answers pertinent questions? The prospect will feel at peace with you when you deal directly with her and understand her needs, wants, and desires. You should consider the relationships you have with customers and think about where it may be beneficial to have a check-in.

- Most important for this process is to actively listen to the customer and repeat back some of their words to them to let them know they have been heard.

Avoid Pitfalls

- Try to avoid making assumptions. Instead, assess. Assess a customer's situation by asking what his or her challenges are.

- Another thing to avoid is going into sales mode too soon. Instead, get to know the prospect's needs first.

Maintenance Check

- Maintain a listening stance to the customer so you can truly understand their business needs. Remember, the more he talks, the more information you will gain. Your job is to listen.

- Address a potential customer's specific situation and use their words when you talk about a solution.

- Leverage a CRM system like Salesforce or Honor Services Office to document and manage the relationship.

- Maintain your calm as you gather information and probe. Remember, you're heading toward a mutually beneficial solution.

Dual Advancement Sales Process™

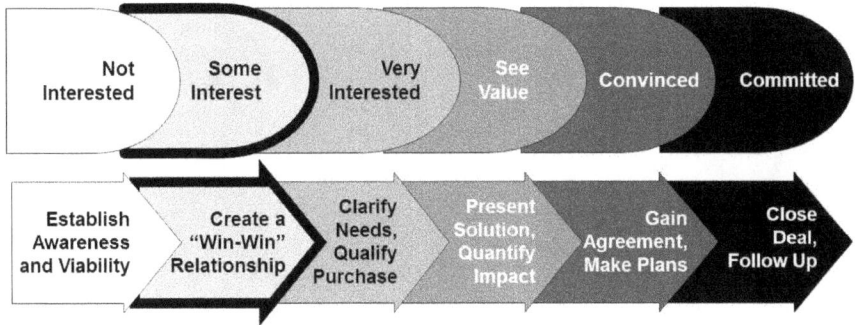

| Not Interested | Some Interest | Very Interested | See Value | Convinced | Committed |

| Establish Awareness and Viability | Create a "Win-Win" Relationship | Clarify Needs, Qualify Purchase | Present Solution, Quantify Impact | Gain Agreement, Make Plans | Close Deal, Follow Up |

Dual Process Step 2: Create a Win-Win Relationship

It's great to do business with someone you trust. I (Dan) remember a time when the muffler on my car was making so much noise, I was sure that it needed to be replaced. I took it to the shop around the corner from my house, expecting to pay $99 for the new muffler as advertised. The mechanic called me into the shop less than five minutes after I arrived and pointed out that a screw had fallen from one of the parts. He replaced it and the car was ready to go. He only charged me $10. I so appreciated his honesty, I've referred at least 20 people to him. He has a customer for life because he created a win-win relationship.

Partner or Predator?

How do you establish a relationship? When you meet someone you really get along with, you probably make plans to meet again. Perhaps you call to chat. You go into the relationship thinking ahead and wanting to be positive. Approach every customer with the intent of creating a valuable and long-term relationship. Let customers know that your success is directly tied to their success. Work to establish a partnership that is a win for you and a win for them. If you are trying to sell to a customer, he may feel guarded or suspicious of you, because he doesn't know whether or not you are truly trying to help or if you may be taking advantage of him. However, if you are helping him, if you are providing a solution to his problem and he knows for sure that your success is tied to his success, you will create a bond that will lead to a mutually beneficial relationship.

For example, on *The Shark Tank* (season 3, episode 9, which featured a sales distribution method for a stand-up paddle board), Dallas Mavericks owner Mark Cuban turned from a shark to a salesperson. He saw potential in an entrepreneur and made a fair offer for the entrepreneur's business that Mark was not that excited about, with an gentleman's agreement that the business owner would give Mark the first right of refusal for other products he would develop. It was a true win-win relationship. If Mark had tried to be a predator (like most of the sharks), then the entrepreneur probably wouldn't have accepted his offer and both people would have lost out on a great opportunity.

When you are establishing a relationship with your customer, remember to think about doing things that will establish trust and create long-term value for both of you. It will be a better benefit for everyone.

Customer Mindset: Some Interest

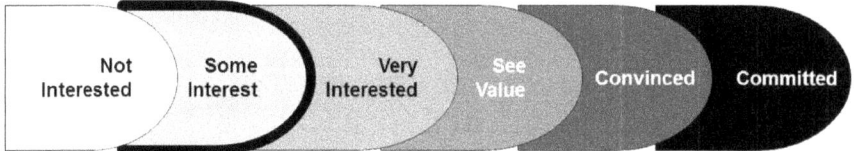

| Not Interested | Some Interest | Very Interested | See Value | Convinced | Committed |

On-the-Fence Prospects

Some Interest is an exciting yet very dangerous period of the sale. The customer has a general understanding of your product or service and knows that you can potentially help her, yet she is not fully sold.

This is the time to have the patience of a Venus fly trap. This delicate plant waits patiently before it clamps its prey in a vice grip hold. We want you to have the patience part rather than the death grip part.. I (Stan) ignored the on-the-fence prospect and thought they were moving along with me, only to find they were buying from someone else. Some on-the-fence prospects:

Ambivalent. Prospects at this stage do not care one way or another. The benefits and value of your product or service haven't fully sunk in. Building the relationship as the expert is more important than being their pal. Provide assistance from a professional stance. Ambivalent prospects need facts related to the benefits of your product or service.

Postponed. This prospect has temporarily called off the search because of various reasons. Sending benefits and facts to this person could be detrimental. Find out what's wrong and reach out to them to offer assistance. This will be an opportunity for you to build a trusting relationship by aiding a person who is in need. Work within your boundaries.

Closed. You can't win 'em all. Expect some people to choose another product or service. This is not personal or uncommon. Respect their wishes to be removed from your email list and move on.

I (Dan) know that I cannot sell my product or service to everyone. I have to remember that I am seeking the people who will say yes. Some people may not be ready for my solution at this moment. There will be some who will never leverage my services. This is a time to stay encouraged and keep moving forward.

Consultative Sales Step: Create a Win-Win Relationship

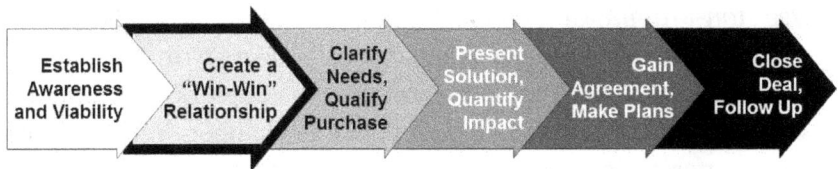

Establish Awareness and Viability	Create a "Win-Win" Relationship	Clarify Needs, Qualify Purchase	Present Solution, Quantify Impact	Gain Agreement, Make Plans	Close Deal, Follow Up

This is the second phase in the Dual Process. Now that you have met your prospects and they are aware of your company, it is time to customize the benefits statements of your product or service. In this phase, you develop the foundation for a mutually beneficial relationship by gaining an understanding of the customer and what they need for success.

Analyze Decision Makers

Whether you are speaking to one person in a group or a large company, it is important to know who the decision maker is. I (Stan) once spent a significant amount of time meeting with a person I thought was the decision maker. We developed solutions and had some great conversations. When it seemed like we had a deal, he said, "I have to ask my boss." I had to start over.

Here are some suggestions to help you analyze potential decision makers:

Develop a Decision-Maker Matrix. Create a spreadsheet listing all of your prospects at the company of interest. List their name, title, and decision-making status. Statuses include *decision maker, influencer, connector,* or *future prospect.* Note that I did not include *time waster,* because everyone you meet is a prospect or a customer.

Some sales opportunities open and close in one conversation and may not need a decision-maker matrix.

Gather Needs Early. Peaceful selling is inquisitive. The more questions you ask regarding your customers' needs the better. Needs can sound like complaints. For example, "I'm tired of keeping track of financials" may prompt you as the salesperson to think of solutions that would enable automated bookkeeping.

Decision-Making Calendar. Develop a decision-making calendar listing the dates of the decision-making process within the company to which you are selling. For example, the Federal Government has a sales cycle that begins in July and ends in October. Various groups hold conferences on certain dates that you would list on this calendar.

Analyze Moving Forward. After gathering the list of decision makers, their decision-making process, and their needs, determine whether moving forward is worth the effort by doing a *Strengths, Weaknesses, Opportunities, and Threat (S.W.O.T.) analysis.* Document the strengths and weaknesses of the relationship and how your product or service matches the discussed problem. Document the financial opportunity as well as any other intangibles such as relationship building or goodwill. List any threats you may have regarding the sale.

This visual helps you decide if pursuing the sale is worth it.

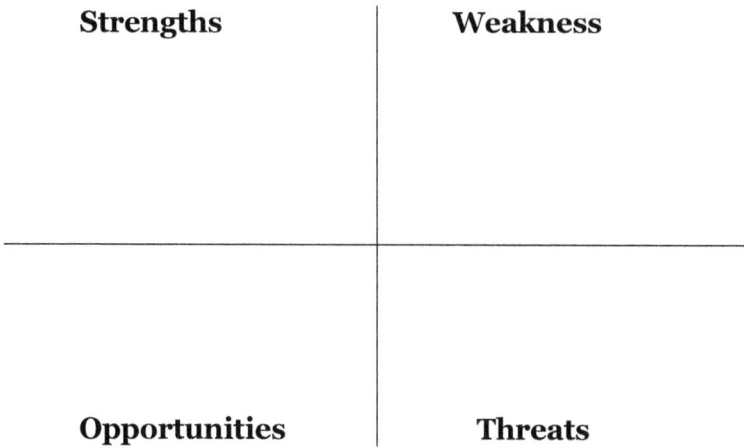

Strengths	**Weakness**
Opportunities	**Threats**

The more strengths and opportunities you list, the more feasible it is to move forward with the sales process.

Develop Preliminary Benefits Statements. Leverage your knowledge of your product and service to tailor benefits statements specific to your customer. For example, when speaking to a track runner, a shoe salesperson may say, "This shoe will give you exquisite grip on the turns (referring to the curves in the track)." The salesperson would then tailor the benefits statement to the walker: "This shoe will enable you to walk long distances, supporting your arch along the way."

Relationship Check-In

- Let's revisit our car dealer in previous chapters. By identifying the customer's needs, the dealer could develop a solution that is satisfactory for all parties.

- Realize that you, the salesperson, should not lose, nor should the customer. Since your customer is purchasing, they must feel they received great value. By identifying the customers' needs you will gain peace in knowing how to tailor your solutions to fit their needs.

Avoid Pitfalls

- Be careful not to assume that your customer knows the value of your product or service. Offer information to help inform your customer.

- Avoid jumping in with solutions without fully understanding the problem. You may miss out on additional sales opportunities.

- Sometimes the customer may want to jump ahead to your solution. The danger here is that he may like what you have, but may not know all of your capabilities. At this point, it is important to guide them through the process.

Maintenance Check

- Add a reminder to speak to decision makers during the decision-making cycle. Tools like Outlook and Honor Services Office have places where you can add automatic reminders.
- Provide the decision maker with credible solutions to real problems.
- Consider what's in it for you and what the value is to the customer to gain a win-win.
- Explain your value from the customer's perspective.
- Objectively evaluate whether it is worth your time to pursue this opportunity.
- Be willing to walk away.

Dual Advancement Sales Process™

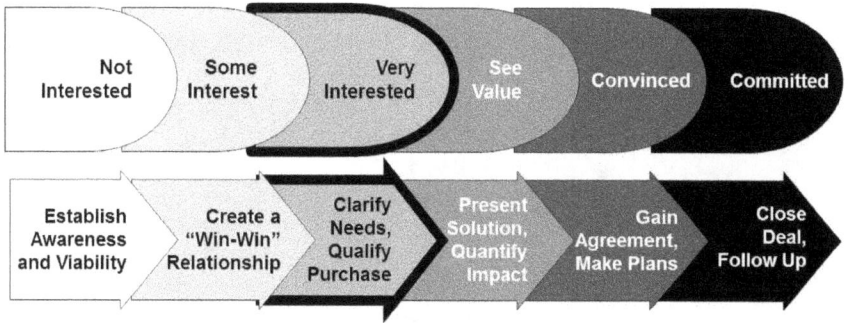

Not Interested	Some Interest	Very Interested	See Value	Convinced	Committed

Establish Awareness and Viability	Create a "Win-Win" Relationship	Clarify Needs, Qualify Purchase	Present Solution, Quantify Impact	Gain Agreement, Make Plans	Close Deal, Follow Up

Dual Process Step 3: *Clarify* Their Needs and *Qualify* Their Ability to Purchase

Many of us have heard a doctor say, "Tell me where it hurts. . . . Do you have insurance?" A good doctor will make the effort to fully understand your medical situation before prescribing any medication. She will check your vital signs, assess your pain level, and ask how the trouble started. During the consultation, she will also make sure you can pay for it! A good doctor also helps patients who aren't sure what they're going through to understand the nature of their pain.

A good salesperson does the same thing a doctor does. A good salesperson strives to understand a customer's situation, challenges, and plans to address the challenges (or how not being able to address those challenges impacts them). Last, but not least, a good salesperson makes sure the customer can pay for services rendered.

Customer Mindset: Very Interested

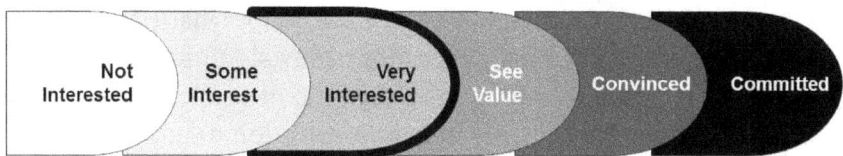

Not Interested | Some Interest | Very Interested | See Value | Convinced | Committed

By now the customer should know that you have a solution that will meet their needs. They should be willing to give more detailed information to enable you to better understand their situation and customize that solution for them. Let's explore this mindset more.

Excited/Inquisitive. When your customer is excited, they will ask you questions and engage you in conversations. Be ready with answers to follow-up questions, along with a few questions of your own to gain clarity. Asking more questions tends to engage the inquisitive person and shows you are trying to clarify the statements.

Prove It! This person is headed in a direction toward your product or someone else's. They lump the burden of proof in your lap and now it is time for you to shine. Provide facts, testimonials, test results, and other pertinent information for this person. Make them feel at ease by helping them toward an understanding of the solutions you can provide.

Backslider. This person is resistant to change. They know the facts, but may be afraid of the effort or responsibility changes engender. They may fear they will be fired if a change is made. It is within your power to provide a peaceful solution for this person. Assure them that the product or service will work or will make them seem more productive. As a result, they will look good for having chosen your product or service.

I (Dan) know when I meet a prospect who is not fully sold on the concepts I am presenting. I seek to put them at ease by engaging them in conversations relating to them and their needs. I remember a friend of mine who was interested in hiring me as his personal success coach. He didn't fully understand the value of what a coach could do, so I had to ask him some questions that could help enlighten him. I also shared some examples of what I had done for some other clients. I finally told him to envision himself being as happy as ever and living the exact life that he really wanted to live. Then I told him that I could help him start doing that immediately. He finally got it. He signed up and within two weeks he made a major career change, increased his net income, and dropped 40 pounds within a year. When you focus on customers' needs, they want to buy from you.

Consultative Sales Step: *Clarify* Their Needs and *Qualify* Their Ability to Purchase

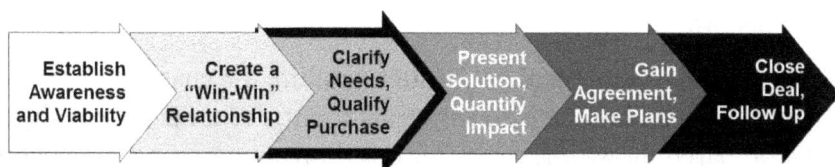

| Establish Awareness and Viability | Create a "Win-Win" Relationship | Clarify Needs, Qualify Purchase | Present Solution, Quantify Impact | Gain Agreement, Make Plans | Close Deal, Follow Up |

At this point in the process, your "very interested" customer is on the cusp of the close. Your part in the process is to identify and agree to the requirements that need to be satisfied in order for the customer to achieve their goals. Once the needs are clarified, it's time to gain an agreement that if you provide a solution, they will buy it from you. At the end of this chapter is a checklist you can use as you implement this step in the process.

Guide Customer through the Funnel

Even a very interested customer might need help to navigate through her expectations and needs in order to advance toward a successful close. Here's how you can use your expertise to guide a customer through this stage.

Obtain Customer Expectations. It is important to learn your potential customers' expectations for a few reasons. First, this helps you learn whether or not these expectations can be met. For example, if someone buying a car were to say they wanted a car that seats eight people, goes from zero to 60 in six seconds, and gets 50 miles to the gallon, you know that you will need to educate that person or walk away, since that product doesn't exist. Second, you'll want to make sure that you are both on the same page so that the customer is not disappointed later.

Align Expectations with Your Product or Service. One easy way to do the alignment is to understand key words from the customer's statement. Listen for words that translate to features or functions of your product or service. For example, if you were selling a computer and you knew that the customer liked to stream movies, you would talk about how much memory the computer has and the state of the art speakers in order to emphasize how that would make watching those movies so much better. It is a lot easier to set yourself up for success by guiding customers to describe features your product or service would satisfy.

Qualify Ability to Purchase. Understanding the customer's budget is an art. One technique is to ask straight out, "What is your budget?" Be prepared, however, since this question sometimes scares people away. Another technique is to make your customer feel at ease by providing options and price ranges they can comfortably fall into. Let them know your top two or three products or services and ask them if their budget fits the range.

Understand Their Timeline to Purchase. Will the customer purchase now or six months from now? You will need to understand timeframes so you can leverage them in your gap analysis.

Stress PAIN. Like the patient described at the beginning of this chapter, sometimes your customer does not know they are hurting. It is important for you to ask questions to emphasize their Problems, Anxieties, Insecurities and Needs (PAIN). Understand what is bothering them and then empathize with their situation. This technique is most effective if you gain a deeper knowledge of their PAIN at a personal and professional level. When you know what bothers them at a personal level, their level of emotion increases, which will increase the likelihood of them doing business with you. Their PAIN is going to help you get paid!

There are few things you can do to uncover a prospect's PAIN.

- **Understand a Customer's Desired State.** The grass is always greener, or at least that is what your customer may be thinking as you discover more about their PAIN. Understand where they would like to be and how soon they would like to get there. Create a desired state note in your CRM.

- **Highlight Wants and Desires.** Need moves your customer to change, but they base their purchase on their wants. For example, you may need a new car, but you want a Mercedes. Be prepared to be more descriptive about your product or service. For example, instead of saying, "Go stay at a hotel and pay money," include descriptions that express a customer's desires. "Get away on your dream vacation in luxurious accommodations to make your stress melt away." Create a wants and desires note in your CRM.

- **Foster a Sense of Urgency.** Many times the situation may be critical for the customer and they may not be aware how their PAIN could turn catastrophic. I (Stan) went to a tire store for some tires. Quite honestly, I knew something was wrong when my car swerved on moist streets. The tire salesman showed me just how bald my tires were and said I could have killed myself and others if I did not purchase tires immediately. I bought four tires. Add a note about dates or timeframes in your CRM.

- **Enable Customer Ownership of the Gap.** Your customer has given you a current state and a desired state in which you have shown there is a gap between their needs and desires versus being settled and satisfied. This is known as the *Gap*. In order for the customer to move closer to the sale, they should own the gap. For example here is a conversation between a weight-loss coach and a customer:

Customer: I would like to lose weight.

Weight Loss Coach: How much weight would you like to lose?

Customer: Oh, about 40 pounds.

The next question is to increase or solidify ownership of the gap.

Weight Loss Coach: And what will this do for you?

Customer: I want to fit into my clothes and feel healthier.

Weight Loss Coach: Fitting into clothes makes everyone feel comfortable and losing 40 pounds makes people feel healthy and confident. I'm sure we can help you reach your goal.

The customer has just expressed ownership and the salesperson has successfully mirrored the gap ownership.

Do a Conditional Close. See if the prospect is willing to buy from you. This is what is called a "conditional close." You ask them if that if you provide the solution for them, do they intend to purchase from you. If they say no, then you can clarify why not or decide if you want to move forward. Either way, you need to know what their intention is or you may waste a lot of time and resources.

Ask Impact Questions. The better you can clarify where a potential customer is now (and help them understand their PAIN), the more you will increase their desire to change. The more you can show how your product will make a positive impact, the more you will increase their desire. For example: If someone were thinking about buying a dishwasher, you would want to highlight the challenges they currently face. You should ask questions about how much time they spend washing dishes, how washing dishes by hand every day would mess up their hands and nails, how dirty dishes can be an eyesore in the sink, etc. Then you would talk about how easy it is with a dishwasher, how much time they could save, how their kitchen would look cleaner, etc.

✔ Relationship Check-In

- Just like a doctor, you have to truly understand your customer's pain. Some pain, if it has been around awhile, becomes tolerable, but at what costs? Just as a doctor explains the seriousness of the ailment, you the salesperson must explain the pain of missed opportunity, possible fines, loss of sales, decrease in quality, and other issues that could arise. Help your customer or prospect gain a sense of peace by warning them of the consequences they can avoid.

Clarify Their Needs and Qualify Their Ability to Purchase Checklist

☐ Get a prospect's full vision for success.

Ask questions to understand what their idea of success is. Here are a few examples:
- What is your vision for success? What does success look like for you?
- How is success measured?
- What would be ideal?
- What do you want?
- What is your vision for how you want you department to be?

☐ Ask questions to emphasize their Problems, Anxieties, Insecurities, and Needs (PAIN).

By understanding a prospect's situation and problems, you can highlight them later and empathize to partner. Here are a few examples:
- What are your challenges?
- What do you like or not like about "X"?
- Tell me about the service/productivity that you are currently receiving. What is working? What isn't working?
- What is the biggest risk that you currently have?
- What happens when something goes wrong?
- What happens when things don't go as smoothly as they should? How does that impact you?

☐ Gain a fuller understanding of where the customer is now and the gap to their success.

Make an effort to quantify where they are right now versus where they could be in an ideal situation. They should understand their discomfort with their current state and desire to change. Here are some examples:
- So, where are you now vs. where you would like to be?

- On a scale from 1 to 10, how would you rate where you are now? (Make the gap as broad as possible!)
- Ask Cost, Quality, Convenience (simple, adaptable, etc.), Impact questions such as, "How much are you spending on this service now?" "What does it cost to maintain?" "How much time does it take to do? "What problems do you have with it?"

☐ Mutually agree upon the gap (the customer's needs) and the value to them for achieving success.

These questions are designed to transition from the way the solution would impact their business to how it may impact them on a personal level. The more people benefit personally, the more inclined they are to choose that solution.

- What impact does this gap have on your department?
- How would things be different if you implemented a change?
- What impact would this solution have on you?
- How much time would it save?
- How would this solution be better for you?

☐ Consider these questions as you explore your potential customer's gap.

The following are questions that can lead to a good perspective on your customer's needs and how they impact him or her.

- Cost: How much will the solution save? Include process time, etc.
- Quality: How will the solution save time? Provide more accurate results? Increase reliability?
- Convenience: Will the solution make my product easier to use? More adaptable? Reduce noise?
- Personal Impact: By saving time, will it reduce stress? Free up more time for me to spend with my family?
- Productivity: Will it increase productivity? Provide faster results?

☐ Make sure the customer has the authority and resources to pursue the solution.

Problems occur when selling to someone who can't make the final decision to buy. Make every effort to deal with the decision maker and learn what his or her decision-making process entails.

- What is the normal procedure for making a purchase?
- Who else should be involved (tech, department head, purchasing, spouse)?
- How long does this type of transaction typically take to complete?

☐ Gain the potential customer's agreement that if you can provide the solution, they will buy it.

Find out if the prospect is truly serious about buying from you. You should be sincere and firm when asking these questions:

- If we can provide the solution, will you purchase it?
- Is there any reason why you wouldn't buy this?
- When are you looking to buy?
- What timeframe do you see this being implemented?

⚠ Avoid Pitfalls

- Breezing through the conversations and assuming a prospect is listening can lead to lost sales.
- Ask questions to confirm, rather than assuming you know what the customer needs.
- In the same light, don't assume your customer knows all of the problems they have. It is up to you to ask deeper level questions to help surface ones they may not have considered.
- Blindly excited people may not be working off of facts. They see the glitz and glamour of "new." They can become just as excited about someone else's product or service. That's why

it's best to clarify needs or expectations before committing more time to meeting with a potential customer who is only slightly interested in your product or service.

- Don't assume that all of their problems have the same impact or priority. Get the customer to assign a value to their problems and quantify how your solution would help them.

- Avoid getting to far into the sales process without talking about price. Make sure they know the price range of your solution and are able to pay for it.

- Understand the prospect's timeframe to purchase and the timeframe to pay. Some service-driven industries may take up to three months to remit payments. Be aware of the impact a timeframe will have upon your business before you agree on the work.

Maintenance Check

- Ask questions of your prospects and clarify their PAIN so you can relate to them and provide adequate solutions.

- Make an effort to understand the customer's situation, challenges, and expectations. You should be able to repeat what they told you (using their words as much as possible) and confirm that you got it correct.

- Do a conditional close. Ask them if you can provide the solution, will they buy it?

- Involve the decision maker in the process.

Dual Advancement Sales Process™

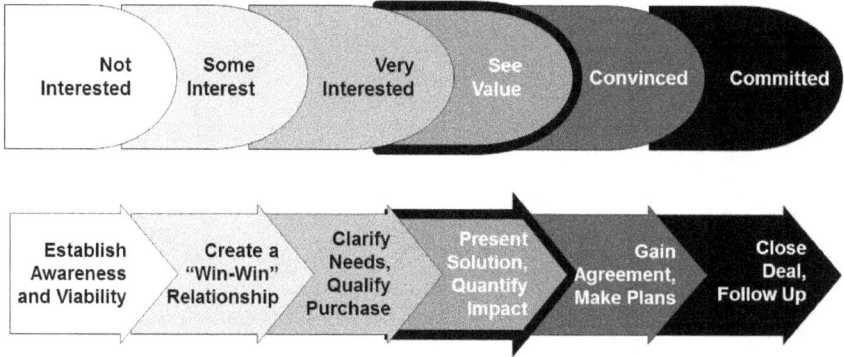

| Not Interested | Some Interest | Very Interested | See Value | Convinced | Committed |

| Establish Awareness and Viability | Create a "Win-Win" Relationship | Clarify Needs, Qualify Purchase | Present Solution, Quantify Impact | Gain Agreement, Make Plans | Close Deal, Follow Up |

Dual Process Step 4: *Present* the Solution and *Quantify* the Impact

Continuing with example in the previous chapter, after the doctor understands what is troubling the patient, he recommends solutions based on the patient's situation: "You've told me what's wrong. Here is what I recommend and here is how you should feel afterwards. How does that sound to you?"

In sales, use the information that you collected to recommend a custom solution to meet a prospect's needs. Additionally, you can take the time to explain the benefits of your solution and the expected outcomes. Even if the solution is simple, the prospect should feel special.

For example, instead of just saying, "Take two aspirin and call me in the morning," a good doctor would say, "You told me you have a headache, so I recommend that you take two aspirin, instead of this other drug because it could upset your stomach. You should feel back to normal in the morning. Call me to let me know how you are. We can decide what to do after that. Is that okay with you?"

Now let's discuss how your tailored solutions can help a character see the value in your product or solution.

Customer Mindset: See Your Value

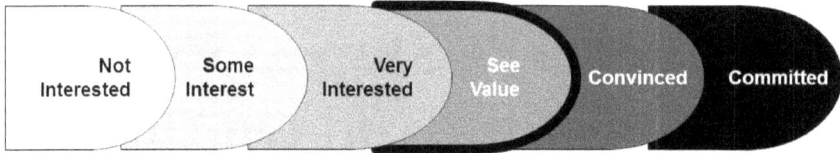

| Not Interested | Some Interest | Very Interested | See Value | Convinced | Committed |

At this stage, the customer has an understanding of your value, but needs to know that you have a solution to their specific problems. Customers tend to fall into one of a few different categories when it comes to seeing your value.

Visionary. Your customer sees value in you, your product, and services. They are now beyond Very Interested and are looking forward to developing solutions with you. Listen for the transition from "I" language to "we" language. This important transition shows a stronger relationship is beginning to form.

Stagnant. This person is difficult to move and could drain a lot of your time. They want change, but keep bringing up barriers that prevent them from moving forward with the process. They may still be Very Interested and may require more gap discussions. Be patient. There is no need to rush this person. Have a pipeline of others who are moving through the process. In the meantime, keep revisiting the stagnant customer.

Leaning. This person is possibly veering off course because of a lack of information, distractions, or miscommunication. It is time for clarity. Personal preference could be getting in the way. Remember, your competition has a sales force too, so mixed messages may be causing confusion.

I (Stan) understand that people resist change, so I remain patient. When I see someone who is stagnant or leaning, I relax and schedule my communication with the prospect in intervals that not only give them room but also keeps our product or service on his radar.

Consultative Sales Step: Present the Solution and Quantify the Impact

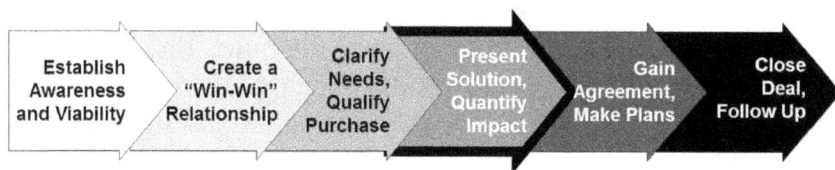

Present the solution using the prospect's language and relating it to the needs that were discussed in the previous step. Afterward, quantify the impact your solution will have on your prospect's business.

I (Dan) feel the PAIN of my prospects. In order to develop the best solution, I put try to put myself in their shoes to fully understand what they are going through. I seek to understand if there are external influences that I can alleviate to assist them in their decision-making process.

Develop a Solution Together

The best way to make sure that a customer chooses your solution is to involve them in creating that solution. As you are putting it together, you can work with them and their staff to make sure it will satisfy their needs. Get feedback along the way and give as many accolades as possible. Once you have created the solution together, you can use the following process to present it to them.

Review the Current State and PAIN. (For more about PAIN, see "Dual Process Step 3.") Revisiting the customer's current situation and agreeing to the problems and challenges that were discussed previously provides clarity to the conversation. This should really be a reminder and confirmation of what you discussed with your customer. After reviewing the customer's situation, check to see if his or her expectations have changed. Clarifying the needs with your customer gets everyone on the same page, so that when you present the solution, everyone will be in agreement. And you could also check to see if any other solutions have been presented by competitors. This will allow you to address any doubts that a competitor may have brought up.

Develop a Proposal or Answer. Leverage as input your prospect's expectations, needs, wants, desires, and timeframes that you previously documented in your CRM. Develop a solution that aligns with your customer's needs as you work together on a solution. Use language that makes him or her feel special. The following tips should help ensure that you are successful at presenting the solution to the customer.

- **Tailor Your Benefits Statements.** Knowledge of your product and service becomes critical at this stage. Match the benefits of features, service levels, value, quality, speed, and avoidance of problems and other items of value to your customers PAIN.

- **Quantify Your Solution.** Quantifying is more than cost. Quantify time savings, speed of the car, hours involved in delivering a quality product, savings or cost avoidance. Align these metrics to what your customer values most. For example, "This bed sheet is made with a thread count of 700 stitches per inch, thus making it softer to sleep on. Therefore, you will get better rest." The impact is important to mention. Impact makes the solution personal to the prospect. In the example the sheet speaks to a deeper desire of not only getting quality bedcovers but also better rest. Be intuitive with impact questions and language.

- **Add or Remove.** Add a *Nibbler* to your solution if you have room. Nibblers are additional items you can add to enhance the solution, provide value, and increase profit. Sometimes it is better to lose a little than to lose a lot. Removing some items from the solution may mean you gain a sale. Be careful not to make this a habit by revisiting your pricing, products, or services.

- **Close the Gap.** Show the prospect that your solution is going to take them from their current state—their state of

PAIN—to a state of comfort and happiness—a state of peace. Ideally, you can show them so many benefits from your solution that they will be convinced you have the best solution and yearn for it.

Relationship Check-In

- Our doctor expresses care and a well-thought-out hypothesis. After understanding the patient's pain and discomfort, the doctor expresses genuine care enough to prescribe the best treatment. Likewise, you can develop the best solution for the prospect from the information you gather as you leverage your probing, mutually beneficial questions.

Present the Solution and Quantify the Impact Checklist

☐ Review your prospect's needs, challenges, problems, wants, and desires.

Here you are checking to see if you and your prospect are still on the same page in regard to the prospect's current situation.
- List all of the needs the prospect mentioned.
- Confirm that the items listed are still needs.
- Ask if there is anything new that your prospect would like to add to the list.
- Ask the prospect to prioritize those needs.
- Confirm the prospect's desired outcome.

☐ Discuss facts, features, and benefits/advantages. (Use evidence or testimonials.)

Laughter is contagious as is excitement. By showing your excitement about what your solution can do for their business, your prospect will in turn become excited.
- Review Need, Feature, Impact and get your prospect's Response. Ask them how they feel about the feature and how it could make a positive difference for them.
- Use evidence or testimonials to support your statements.
- Build the bridge for the gap. (Everything you are saying should build momentum.)

☐ Quantify the impact the solution will have on their business and how it can help them personally.

These questions really focus on how the solution will improve a prospect's life professionally and personally.
- Ask the prospect what impact the solution will have on their business. (Get numbers or percentages if possible—percentage increase, financial impact, etc.)
- **Cost:** How much will your solution save your prospect? Include process time, etc.

- **Quality:** How will your solution improve your prospect's time? Will it provide more accurate results or improve reliability?
- **Convenience:** Is your solution easier to use? More adaptable? Does it reduce noise?
- **Personal Impact:** Will your solution save your prospect time? Reduce stress? Allow more time with his or her family?
- **Productivity?** Will your solution increase productivity? Will it provide faster results?

☐ Ask your prospect confirmation and acknowledgement questions to close the gap.

Remember to get feedback from the prospect. You want him to feel involved. Also you'll want to know that you are on the right track in providing a solution.

- Get your prospect to acknowledge that your solution meets their needs. You might ask the prospect, "Do you agree that this solves your problems?"
- Ask questions to confirm that your solution is the best solution for them.
- Ask your prospect if he has any concerns. Be prepared to handle any objections.

 **Avoid Pitfalls**

- Avoid giving a generic solution off the top of your head. Your prospect will sense the insincerity.

- Do not assume your prospect knows the value of what you presented. Be prepared to explain.

- Be careful not to go into solution mode without getting a fuller understanding of your prospect's needs.

- You don't have to offer more than you can afford in order to make the sale.

- When a prospect provides vague answers, ask for clarification. Walk away with a better understanding. In this way, you can formulate better questions to help your prospect with her need.

Maintenance Check

- Review your prospect's needs and vision in order to present the best solution for the challenges they face.
- Quantify the impact your solution will make on your prospect's business. Tailor the solution to your prospect so they will know how much your solution will benefit them.
- Confirm that your solution solves their problem by having your prospect own the solution of leveraging your product or services.

Dual Advancement Sales Process™

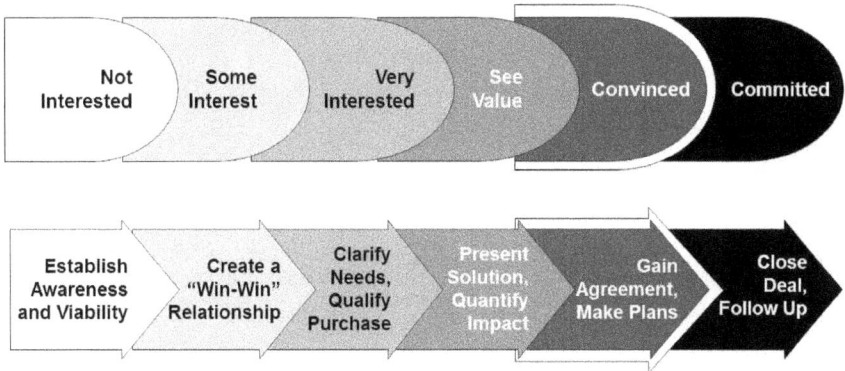

| Not Interested | Some Interest | Very Interested | See Value | Convinced | Committed |

| Establish Awareness and Viability | Create a "Win-Win" Relationship | Clarify Needs, Qualify Purchase | Present Solution, Quantify Impact | Gain Agreement, Make Plans | Close Deal, Follow Up |

Dual Process Step 5: *Gain Agreement* and Make Plans

Before you take a road trip with your family, you would do one final check-in to make sure that everyone is on board, especially your spouse. You may say, "We're going to Disneyland for spring break. Is everyone okay with that? All right, let's start planning." You would then plan what you are going to do and create an itinerary of some sort. The same is true for making the final decision in sales. You need to get an agreement from your prospect that the solution you presented is the best and that they will make plans to implement it. Many deals stall because prospects procrastinate due to the fact that the next step means change. People tend to resist change, no matter how much they know it will help them.

After you gain the necessary agreement, accelerate your prospect's buying process by making plans for when they will purchase and implement the solution. If your prospect can visualize the process of implementation, he or she is more likely to move forward. You can assist by making plans for the implementation.

Customer Mindset: Convinced

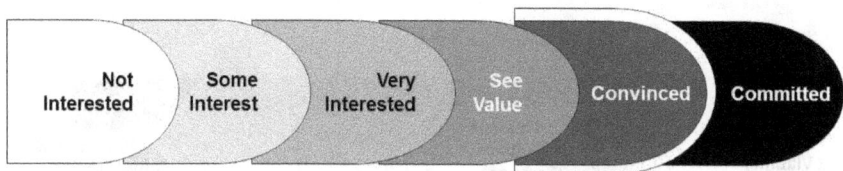

| Not Interested | Some Interest | Very Interested | See Value | Convinced | Committed |

The prospect should know that you have the best solution for their problems. Prospects tend to fall into one of the following categories.

Persuaded. Your prospect completely understands the value of your solution and knows how it will make a positive impact on her business. In order to keep the process moving forward, now is the time to simply suggest that your prospect make plans to buy from you.

Informed. Your prospect understands what your product does and can see how it could work for them, but they may not yet see how your solution is better than a competitor's solution. By referring back to their needs and gap, you can help move them toward a decision by expressing what they need, how you can provide the solution, and what impact that solution will achieve.

Cloudy. Your prospect either has little knowledge of how your product will solve their needs or is leaning towards a solution that is different from what you offer. This deal will probably be very difficult to close. Face your prospect in the same way you dealt with the informed prospect, but ask openly if they see the value of what you provide. Or you could ask them if they are favoring a competitor and then show them how your solution is better. Remember not be combative; rather, be peaceful. By cutting to the chase, you can save anxious moments, wondering if this person is on board or not.

I (Stan) like to review my facts and benefits statements often. This helps me deliver the best information to those who are informed consumers. In these days of online customer reviews and "likes," I have to stay abreast of the latest information regarding products or services that are similar to mine.

Consultative Sales Step: Gain Agreement and Make Plans

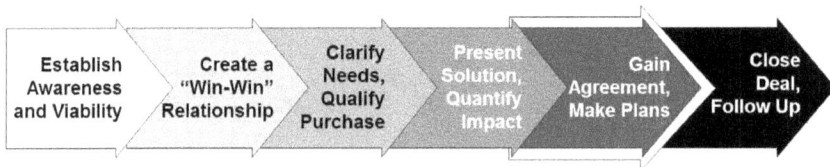

Establish Awareness and Viability | Create a "Win-Win" Relationship | Clarify Needs, Qualify Purchase | Present Solution, Quantify Impact | Gain Agreement, Make Plans | Close Deal, Follow Up

I (Dan) am a planner. I like to discuss solutions that my prospect's needs on a case-by-case basis. I feel each solution should be crafted for the prospect. This requires me to gain agreement so we can make plans together. I've found the following tips to be helpful when making plans with a customer to implement my solution.

Develop an Issues-Resolutions Document. Address any concerns your prospect or customer may have with the presented solution. Keep great notes on what you discussed and be sure to follow up with your commitments to address any concerns. Follow up within 24 hours if at all possible.

Gain Agreement. People resist change. You can aid in the elimination of your prospect's apprehension by reviewing the benefits and their gap to peace. Remember to empathize with their PAIN and have them focus their attention on a desired outcome. It is better to move toward full agreement than to move to the next phase, thinking that you have agreement when you really do not. Gaining an agreement can lead to total customer satisfaction.

Make Plans to Purchase. Depending on the complexity of the prospect, this stage could happen within one step or many. For example, when selling to a large company, you may need to visit the purchasing department to understand procurement and fill out various forms. If selling to an individual, you may ask, "What form of payment do you use?" or "When would you like this delivered?" Making plans with your prospect enables them to take smaller steps toward your solution, thus bringing them closer to their desired peaceful state.

Remove Buyer's Remorse. Reassure your prospect that they are moving in the right direction: closer to their desired state. For example, if you are a travel agent, say to the very tired and stressed-out prospect, "You will enjoy this vacation. It will give you well-needed rest." By affirming the prospect's desires, you convey to the prospect that you are listening and have their best interests in mind.

Gain Agreement and Make Plans Checklist

☐ Address any concerns the prospect may have.

If you have gone through all of the steps, this should be just a review. Clarify that your solution will work and move forward with confidence.
- Confirm that your solution is the best. Remind your prospect why it is the best.
- Review the benefits and impact of implementing your solution.
- Ask if there any additional concerns.

☐ Make sure you have support/agreement at multiple levels.

It is best to have decision makers and influencers involved in order to achieve full collaboration.
- Confirm that everyone who needs to be involved has had input.
- Ask if there is anyone else with whom you would need to talk.

☐ Make plans for placing the order.

This helps prospects think through the process. It also could uncover any potential problems with making the order.
- Ask the prospect to walk through their requirements for securing the order.
- Ask who needs to be contacted/involved to start implementation.
- Check to see whether or not the purchasing department needs to be involved.

☐ Reassure the prospect that he will be satisfied and successful.

This is an opportunity to bring peace to your prospect. Reassurance can make your prospect feel comfortable and confident moving forward. A little reassurance can go a long way.
- Review the benefits one more time.
- Remind the prospect how valuable it will be to close the gap.

Relationship Check-In

- People are generally agreeable, so be careful not to take "I like it" as a commitment that your prospect is willing to purchase. She may be expressing a want versus a need (i.e., "Wow, that's a cool idea"), but may not be on board to purchase.

- If there are multiple decision makers, gain a commitment from each one. Have critical conversations to help you understand their solid commitment level. This is the time to have your last "difficult" conversation. It is better to get everything out in the open now than to move on to the next phase and still have lingering doubt. Be on their side and provide them with peaceful solutions.

Avoid Pitfalls

- Be careful not to accept "We want it" as a commitment. Get them to say "We will buy it" or "We are going to sign the contract."

- Be careful not to deal with a non-decision maker. Make sure you have the key people there to make the final decision.

Maintenance Check

- Follow up on any commitments within 24 hours. If the commitment takes longer, communicate the resolution time.

- Check to see that you have your prospect's agreement that your solution is the one for them.

- Ask if there are any concerns that may prevent your prospect or decision maker from choosing your product.

- Paint a picture for how your solution will work and start the planning process to implement it.

Dual Advancement Sales Process™

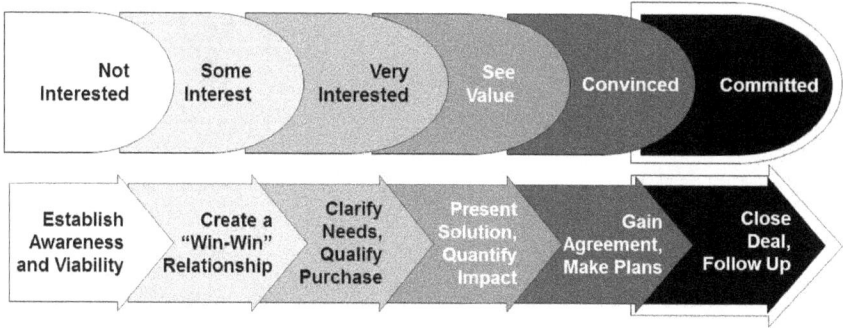

| Not Interested | Some Interest | Very Interested | See Value | Convinced | Committed |

| Establish Awareness and Viability | Create a "Win-Win" Relationship | Clarify Needs, Qualify Purchase | Present Solution, Quantify Impact | Gain Agreement, Make Plans | Close Deal, Follow Up |

Dual Process Step 6: *Close* the Deal and Follow Up!

"I now pronounce you husband and wife." Consider closing the deal to be a marriage, rather than a graduation. A lot of people close a deal and then they feel everything is done. With that philosophy, important opportunities are missed.

If you stop working right after you get married, your marriage won't last! When your customer buys from you, follow up and make sure the customer is using your product or service and is happy with it.

Customer Mindset: Committed

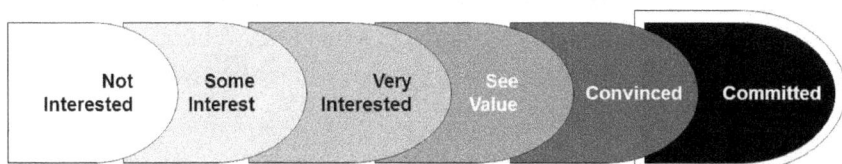

| Not Interested | Some Interest | Very Interested | See Value | Convinced | Committed |

You now have a customer who is committed to you and wants to complete the purchase. At this point, have them sign the agreement and set a date for implementation. On short sales this could happen immediately. Document the next steps. If you are part of a larger organization, confirm the next steps with your team and your customer's team. Check to see that you are able to do everything you commit to doing. Agree to a calendar for being able to check in and follow up.

Committed customers usually fall into one of the following categories.

Committed Customer. This customer is happy with the solution provided and needs very little contact from you. They will call you if they need something. You should follow up with them and their staff maybe once a quarter unless they tell you otherwise.

Positive Reviewer. This is a happy customer who will give you testimonials. They enjoy more contact and will probably want to hear from you regularly. You should contact them once or twice a month or whatever feels appropriate. Set reminders in your CRM to make contact on a semi-regular basis.

Referral Customer. This customer loves your solution and considers you to be part of their team. They will give you testimonials, and probably will allow you to use them for case studies or demonstrations. You should probably be in contact with them weekly or even more frequently.

I (Dan) prefer to take the extra steps to move the customer to the point of referrals. I try to do little things to make my customers feel special. I write handwritten thank you notes and I have sent certificates to those who sat through training on some of the more complex products I have sold. I'll ask them how things are going and if they know someone who could use my services. Where appropriate, I will give them some type of referral reward.

Consultative Sales Step: *Close* the Deal, and Follow Up!

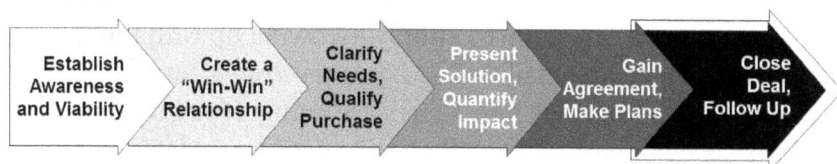

Confidently ask your prospect for the order and close the sale. Sign the paperwork and/or do whatever is necessary to finalize the sale. Follow up with the customer to enhance your relationship and hopefully grow your business.

I (Stan) like to personalize my sales, so I reach out to each of my new customers. I don't want them to feel like they are just a sale. Sometimes I don't have the luxury to communicate to everyone, so I leverage technology where I can and then customize a thank you on the receipt email in an automated fashion. The next few tips are crucial for being able to close the deal effectively and establish ways to follow up in a meaningful manner.

Get a Payment or Signed Agreement/Contract. If you are taking cash, leverage safe cash handling processes as best you can. Look for counterfeit bills especially around holiday seasons. Be careful of taking checks. Leverage "check management" systems through your bank to avoid fraud. Be Payment Card Industry (PCI) compliant when taking credit cards. If you submit or accept invoices, document the payment terms. Is this an immediate payment, Net 15 (15 days from now), Net 30, 60, or 90? Confirm start/ship date. Document all quantities, descriptions, discounts, taxes, and delivery locations.

Deliver Your Product. When it comes to delivery, here is where you can under promise and over deliver. If you can deliver your product or service to them immediately that's great, but what if you have to ship it? State the maximum time and beat it. Your customer will be thankful when your shipment arrives early. Ask to make sure this is agreeable for all concerned, because they may not be available to receive the shipment.

Follow Up with Your Customer. Follow up is what sets a great company apart from a mediocre one. Customer satisfaction is at stake here and you can shine by simply following up with the sale. Make a call or send an email to thank your customer for the purchase. Take time to ask how things are going. If you do this on a regular basis, your customers will provide positive reviews and more importantly, referrals.

Long-Term Follow-Up. Now that you have been communicating on a regular basis with your customer, you can ask for more business by telling them what's new. Offer special deals for long-term customers. Give them sneak peeks and treat this customer as a VIP.

Ask for Referrals and Testimonials. Continue to grow your business through testimonials and referrals. Ask for a testimonial each time, so you can show others that you have quality a great product or service. Remember, the more people who are talking about your business, the more your business will grow.

Relationship Check-In

- I now pronounce you "Closed" and "Committed." Both parties are now experiencing the exhilaration of the sale. Inexperienced salespeople would walk away during this critical stage. Once you have your customer's commitment, you will need to work hard to keep them committed.

- Follow up and make sure your customer is satisfied. This may open the doors for future opportunities, referrals, and new business.

- If at all possible, follow up with your customer to ensure total customer satisfaction. Check with them on any future needs. Establish how to move forward, communicating on a regular basis.

Close the Deal and Follow Up Checklist

Preparation

- ☐ Prospect contacts and/or visits industry references

- ☐ Proposal submitted to prospect and any requested revisions completed

- ☐ Contracts submitted to prospect's legal team for approval

- ☐ Closing date determined

- ☐ Confirmation of implementation team

- ☐ Asked for and resolved objections and concerns

- ☐ Clear vision for success for you and the customer

  Here are key steps to remember:
- ☐ Get a payment or signed agreement/contract. (Confirm start/ship date if necessary.)

  - Formalize the deal with a payment. A verbal agreement and an actual transaction are two different things.
  - Leverage safe cash handling practices.
  - Leverage a PCI Compliant Credit/Debit Solution like Honor Services Office for invoicing.
  - Define payment terms (Immediate, Net 15, 30, 60, 90).
  - Check quantities.
  - Check descriptions.
  - Check discounts.
  - Check applicable state taxes.
  - Check delivery schedule.

- ☐ Deliver your product.

  - Leverage the best shipping for your budget and try to get the product to your customer (if your business involves shipping).
  - If you offer a service, schedule dates for delivery.

☐ Follow up to make sure the product provides the agreed-upon solution.

- It's important to make sure that your customer starts using the product or service and that they are satisfied. You can go back to them for referrals and testimonials later.
- Follow up with different people in the organization to make sure everyone is satisfied.
- You might consider using a customer satisfaction survey to get candid feedback.

☐ Implement a process for long-term follow-up.

- Long-term follow-up is important for your long-term success, especially if you have a recurring service (monthly charges or a product that will need updating after a certain time). If you make sure your customers are happy on an ongoing basis, you will lock out the competition in the future.
- Ask your customer whether or not the process could have been better. This may allow you to develop another product or add-on for the customer.

☐ Look for opportunities for growth with that customer.

- Look for ways you can help your customer's business grow. Chances are, if they grow, they'll use more of your product/services.
- Ask them what you can do to help them grow. Sometimes people need a little nudge in order to expand their business.

☐ Ask the customer for referrals and reciprocate.

- One of the best ways to grow your business is through referrals. Ask for referrals with confidence and reciprocate if you can. (You might give them a thank you gift if appropriate.)
- Ask the customer for testimonials. If you know you are doing well, ask the customer to give you a testimonial that you can share with others. If you aren't doing well, this is your opportunity to do something to earn kudos. Ask what it would take for them to give you a testimonial and do it!

⚠ Avoid Pitfalls

- Do not think the sale is the end of the relationship. (It should be the beginning.)
- Don't be satisfied with only a verbal commitment. Move the customer toward payment without being pushy.
- Keep hot potentials hot by following up leads.
- Keep on the lookout for counterfeit cash or fraudulent checks.

Maintenance Check

- Finalize the deal. Double-check the details.
- Get a safe and secure payment.
- Follow PCI compliant rules if you accept credit cards.
- Agree to follow up with your customers and do it.
- Deliver the value you promised.
- Obtain referrals and testimonials.

Section 3: Executing the Sales Process

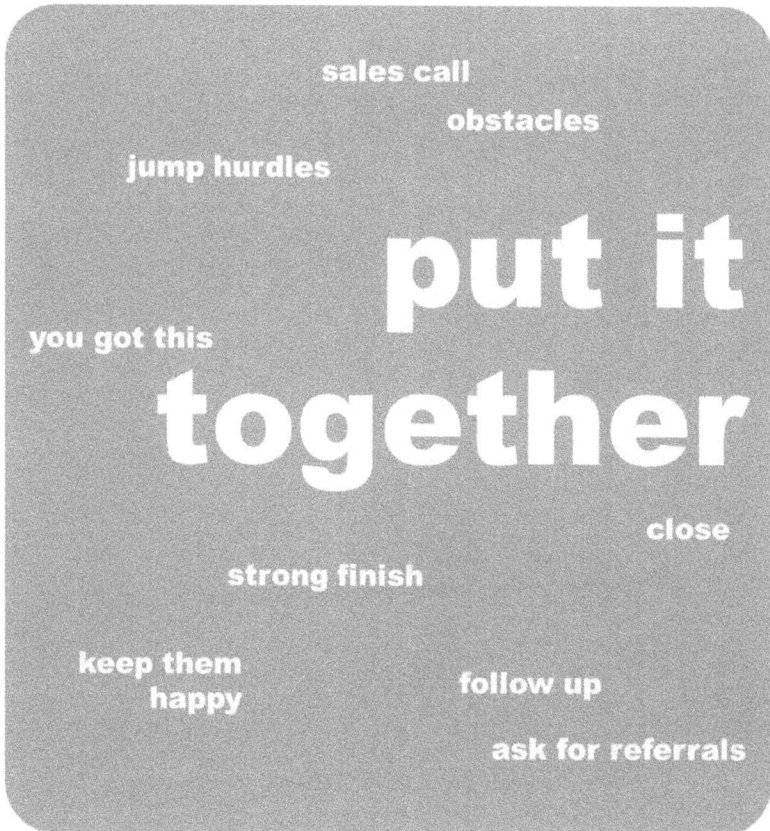

sales call

obstacles

jump hurdles

put it

you got this

together

close

strong finish

keep them
happy

follow up

ask for referrals

Taking the Next Step: Putting the Dual Process into Action

The first part of this book talked about the overall sales process. This process can take place in as little as one meeting, a few meetings, or, in some cases, it can take over a year and include dozens of meetings with various stakeholders. We refer to each meeting as a *sales call*.

There is a certain amount of preparation that can go into each sales call to ensure your success and advance the entire process. We will walk you through the preparation process you can use in your sales calls no matter which phase of the Dual Process you are in. The diagram below explains the actions that should take place to make each sales call successful.

The Sales Call

Prepare

Close & Follow-Up

Open

Sales Call Cycle

Confirm

Engage

Advance

Overcoming Objections

Sales cannot always go without problems. Overcoming objections is a part of the sales process and if done well, could save the sale and most importantly the relationship. In the Overcoming Objections section we will discuss the hurdles you may face and how to overcome them.

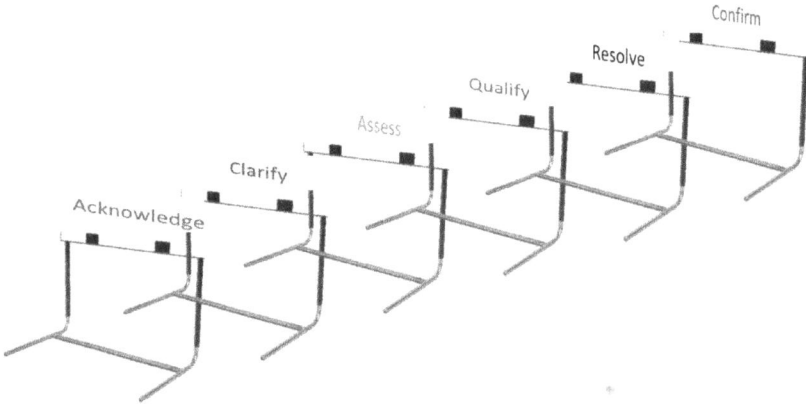

The 6 Hurdles of Overcoming Obstacles

Taking the Next Step: The Sales Call

The journey of a thousand miles begins with a single step.

Chinese **philosopher Lao Tzu** (c 604–531 BC) in the *Tao Te Ching,* chapter 64

Have you ever heard this statement? "I thought *you* knew where the meeting was?" This would indicate that the person probably wasn't prepared for that particular meeting.

Each meeting with a customer/prospect is like a taking a small trip. If you were taking a trip, you would map out your route, make sure you have gas, and do other things to ensure that you reach your destination. The same is true for meeting preparation.

Sales Call Cycle
(Prepare → Open → Engage → Advance → Confirm → Close & Follow-Up)

Before making a sales call, it is important that you know where you are in the sales process, what you expect to achieve, and what value you will deliver for the customer in the call. Review your notes (or research the customer if this is your first meeting with him).

Meeting Step-by-Step Process

Your sales meeting will seem very much like the Dual Sales Process you have just learned. It has an open, content, and close, similar to the fundamental principle for making a speech: tell them what you are going to tell them (open); tell them (content); tell them what you told them (close). Make sure you are progressing your prospect through the entire meeting. Here are a few tips to keep your meetings meaningful.

Prepare for Your Meeting. Prospects can tell when you are winging it, so be prepared. Pull all of your notes together from your CRM and match them to your meeting objective. Make your objective match your sales close cycle. A sales close cycle could be immediate or take place over a year, depending on the size and complexity of your product, so adjust your meeting accordingly.

Since your prospect may not have a lot of time to meet with you, have a clear agenda and meet with them for an appropriate duration. Many meetings are short, but the meeting duration will vary depending on your prospect. Provide directions if you are meeting in person and arrive early. Be sure to communicate enthusiasm. I (Stan) smile when I am on the phone, because my prospects can hear the excitement. If your meeting takes place on the phone, try to keep the conversation brief, purposeful, and free of background noises.

Physical preparation is important for your meeting to be successful. Equally important is the mental preparation for a meeting. One thing I (Dan) do to prepare is to visualize myself conducting the meeting the way I want it to happen. I envision myself guiding the customer through any difficulties that may arise and ultimately having a successful meeting. I find the following tips to be helpful for actually conducting the meeting

Open the Meeting. It is important for you to set the tone for the meeting. Have good energy, project confidence, and let the customer know you are going to guide the meeting. Whenever I open a meeting, I like to review the agenda and collect expectations. If the prospect is reluctant, my approach is to check the appropriate sales step and adjust my questions to see if they are committed with moving forward with the meeting.

Engage Your Prospect. Each step of the Dual Process is different, so review where you are in the process to engage your prospect. This is where I ask questions to assess where my prospect is. I then leverage my preparation of benefits to tailor my statements appropriately to their needs. It is also helpful to review anything that was previously discussed and make sure that nothing has changed. This will help them remain engaged in the process and should avoid any misunderstandings later on.

Advance the Process. Believe it or not, it takes practice to remember to advance the process. I used to think I could sit back and let my prospect decide on whether or not to purchase from me. Now I formally check to see where my prospect is in the process and purposefully advance the process with the Dual Process steps. This helps me relax and remember the goal of bringing my prospect along to commitment rather than pushing a sales transaction and losing. This could be another place where you do a trial close. Ask your prospect: "If I provide a solution, will you buy from me?"

Confirm What Was Said. My prospects love when I listen, so I use mirror language to confirm what was said. I repeat the prospect's needs, wants, desires, current state, and desired state to them so they can understand that I am here to assist them in solution development. The example of the car salesman shows a good way to do that: "So if I can show you a car that looks nice, gets good gas mileage, has a smooth ride and comes in under $400 a month, that would make you happy?" The customer needs to know that they have been heard, and it allows you to confirm that you are clear about what they want.

Close the Meeting and Follow Up. The end of the meeting is one of the most important parts. In closing a meeting, it is a good practice to (1) review what was discussed, (2) confirm the next steps and who has accountability, (3) ask if there are any questions or concerns, and (4) confirm that you are on the right track to providing a solution that your customer will purchase. If possible, I would like to close the sale, but if it is not the appropriate time, I thank the prospect for his or her time and make sure that I follow up as promised. I generally try to have at least one item on my to-do list that I can respond to within 24 hours so that I can continue to build credibility. This gives me an opportunity to check back with the prospect as soon as possible.

Sales Call Cycle Checklist

☐ **Prepare for Your Meeting.** Prepare for each call so you can take the lead and guide the conversation.

- Dual Sales Process step determined
- Long-term objective understood
- Call notes checked
- Responsibilities reviewed and questions determined
- Achievement objective defined
- Objections and concerns anticipated and answers prepared
- Experiential objective defined (How do you want the customer to feel?)

Setting Appointment
- Initial contact made (phone call, email, in-person visit, etc.)
- Pre-qualification completed
- Appointment scheduled
- Researched prospect to determine needs
- Meeting agenda and requirements sent to prospect

Assume that you will be in control of the meeting. It's up to you to have an agenda (or confirm with the customer that they are setting it).

☐ **Open the Meeting.** Set the tone and clarify the agenda with your prospect.

- Set the tone for the meeting based on your experiential objective.
- State the purpose.
- Clarify the agenda and topics for the meeting.
- Confirm the customer is on board and agree to move forward.

Initial Presentation
- Final qualification completed (Prospect is a true opportunity.)
- Prospect's needs assessed
- Decision maker identified
- Purchasing process and requirements identified

- Next steps determined (scheduled a second meeting, collected RFP requirements, etc.)

☐ **Engage Your Prospect.** Make sure the prospect is involved and you both know the customer's needs, PAIN, and benefits.

- Do an appropriate benefits statement and confirm that the customer is on board.
- Review the customer's situation and see if they have any new concerns or challenges.
- Assess whether or not anything has changed.
- Review the to-do lists (if necessary) from the previous meeting.

Information Collecting
- Prospect priorities, issues, and requirements have been documented. (You know their PAIN, anxiety, or discomfort.)
- You have agreed to the customer's top priorities.
- Competitor comparative strengths and weaknesses have been assessed.
- Prospect's internal advocate(s) have been identified.
- Prospect's internal opponent(s) have been identified.
- The purchasing process has been documented and approved.
- Sales team and other collaborators have been briefed.
- Project funding has been applied for and approved.

☐ **Advance the Process.** Show the prospect that you can deliver value by providing solutions to their problems.

- Address the customer's situation by exploring their needs, wants, concerns, challenges, and frustrations.
- Review the customer's list of needs.
- Check to see if consequences exist.
- Explain benefits or prepare benefits statements.
- Understand what options exist. What solutions are available for them?
- Present the solution to their issue (if you are at the appropriate step in the Dual Process).

☐ **Confirm What Was Said.** Summarize what was covered in the meeting and confirm value in moving forward.

- Summarize the call and leverage your CRM to document what was said.
- Confirm that you can add value to the customer with your solution.
- Confirm that the customer will make a decision or take some other action.

☐ **Close and Follow Up.** Agree to the next steps and accountability. (Who, what, and by when?) Follow through on your commitment.

- Confirm the next steps for you and the customer.
- Decide on a meeting date and time.
- Confirm any other action items.
- Start working on your next call sheet.

A well-executed sales call will enhance your relationship, establish you as the expert, and increase your value to your customer. Remember to keep progressing towards success by getting to know your customer so you can provide the best solution possible.

Avoid Pitfalls

- Be careful not to get derailed by your customer or surroundings. Keep the topic focused on the matter at hand in a friendly way.
- Avoid dominating the conversation and making assumptions. Instead, be ready with questions to learn more about your prospect.

Maintenance Check

- Listen for gold nuggets you can use to develop a great solution.
- Be on time and be present during the conversation.
- Have an agenda and specific goals.
- Use mirror language when you can, repeating what your customer said in your own words.

Taking the Next Step: Overcoming Objections

Objections Are Hurdles, Not Barriers

Edwin Moses has one of the longest winning streaks in sports history, because he learned how to run the 400-meter hurdles better than anyone during his era. He developed a technique for overcoming each hurdle. You can do the same for any objection!

In order to be successful in sales, you must be able to overcome objections. If you learn to welcome objections and accept them as a normal part of the sales process, then you can dominate your competition and achieve success beyond your wildest dreams. As part of the Peaceful Selling philosophy, we believe you can also handle objectives in a peaceful manner. We developed the following six-step process to help you address and overcome any objection.

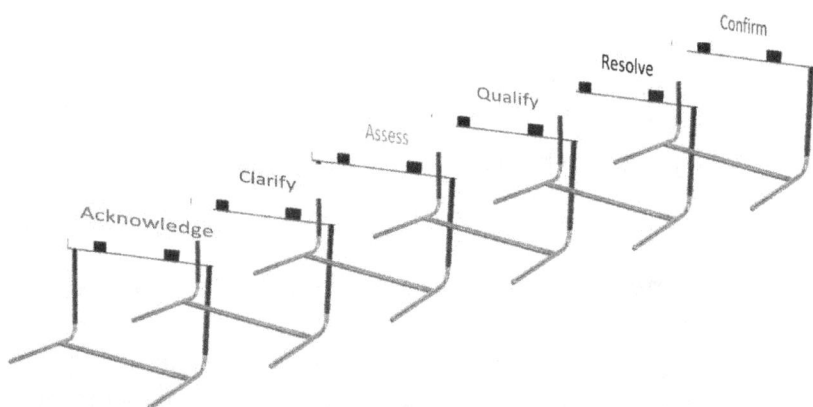

Here is the process of overcoming barriers:

1. Acknowledge the Barrier or Objection. You want to acknowledge the objection and help your objecting prospect feel valued, prudent, and smart for bringing up objections. It's also important to recognize that some people may bring up an objection just to feel involved or valued. This makes acknowledging the objection even more important.

Objections can be your opportunity to shine and show the potential client that you really know your stuff! And it's better to have the objections up-front so that you can address them now, rather than at the end where they can delay or derail a sale. Avoid being defensive.

2. Clarify the Barrier or Objection. Here is where mirror language will become important. By repeating what was said, you let your prospect know you are listening and you will be able to address the gap. I (Dan) can sense when my prospect has objections, but sensing is not enough. I probe to see if my prospect has any objections or barriers to moving forward. I remain calm while addressing the issue expeditiously. I expect the unexpected at each step in the process so I am ready when wrong things occur.

3. Assess the Situation. After gaining clarity, assess the situation by prioritizing the objections in a list. The more objections, the more clarification of benefits you may need to present. Again, do not be defensive or too reactive; rather, be inquisitive and use mirror language to begin the resolution process. Here are a few tips:

- **Don't Stop at the Objection.** Don't let an objection derail your motivation. Understand the underlying reason behind the objection. What is the deeper impact that the customer is truly concerned about? (You may prioritize if they have several.)

- **Combine Acknowledge, Clarify, and Assess.** Check whether this is a fair objection, thank your prospect for bringing it up and make sure that you fully understand, what their objection is.. Say a little more about the impact to their situation.

Below are a number of possible objections and solutions you can use as examples to objections you may experience..

Objection: The solution will cost more than it does.

Solution: Show that the actual cost is within budget.

Objection: The prospect can't afford that expenditure in one year.

Solution: Propose several payments over two or more years.

Objection: The prospect's budget is tight.

Solution 1: Show them more savings as a result of the product. Their bottom line is more profit.

Solution 2: Show that more revenue generated. The bottom line is more profit.

Objection: The prospect will have to pay overtime to implement the solution.

Solution: Extend the implementation so overtime will not be necessary.

4. Qualify and Quantify the Objection. Understand the gap between your solution and what the customer is objecting to. Understand quantities as well as qualities that are missing or not agreed upon. And, you may want to assess how important that issue is to your customer. You can simply ask how high of a priority it is or ask her to rate the importance on a scale of 1 to 10, etc.

5. Resolve the Issue. This is the most important part of handling the objection. The most effective approach to resolving the issue is to be direct with the customer about how you are going to solve the problem. Repeat the objection and tell your customer how you will solve it. You can also let them know you will develop a plan to resolve the issue. Do what is necessary to address the objection. The chart below is a good example of the more common objections you may face and an effective option for how you can address them.

Objection	Resolution
• Misunderstanding	• Provide clarification.
• Uncertainty	• Provide proof.
• Minor drawback	• Show the big picture.
• Actual obstacle	• Take action.

6. Confirm That the Process Is Still Moving Forward. After you respond, it is crucial to confirm with the client that the objection has been handled. This lets them know that they have been heard and that they are valued.

By resolving your potential customer's objections and confirming that they feel comfortable moving forward, you have an opportunity to gain your prospect's confidence in your solution.

Overcoming Objections Checklist

☐ **Acknowledge the Objection.** Support a prospect's willingness to object and thank them for it. Here are some statements you can use to show your support.

  ■ Thanks for bringing it up.
  ■ Thanks for your candor.
  ■ That's a fair question.
  ■ I can tell that you are thorough.
  ■ Let's talk about that.
  ■ Let me think about that for a moment.
  ■ You may be right.
  ■ I want you to be completely comfortable/satisfied.

☐ **Clarify the Barrier.** Make sure you understand the objection. Use clarifying language when you address the objection.

Sample Statements
  ■ I want to make sure that I have it correct. What is your concern?
  ■ It sounds like you are concerned about . . .

☐ **Assess the Situation.** Assess the value/priority of the objection. Gain agreement to move forward if you resolve the objection.

Sample Statements
  ■ Help me understand. I've got in my mind why that might be important, but can you explain ____?
  ■ What makes that an issue for you?
  ■ Tell me more about that.
  ■ How does that impact you?
  ■ How important is that to you?
  ■ Exactly what is bothering you so much about this?
  ■ Can you explain that one more time for me?

☐ **Qualify and Quantify the Objection.** Make sure that when you address the objection, you will be able to move forward.

Sample Statements
- So if we resolve this, will that make you comfortable enough to move forward?
- If we can't resolve this objection now, can we agree to get back to it at another time?
- Is this a deal breaker if we can't resolve this?
- On a scale from 1 to 10, how important is this to you?

☐ **Resolve the Issue.** Address the objection with confidence.

Repeat the objection and tell your customer how you will solve it.

Objection	Resolution
• Misunderstanding	• Provide clarification.
• Uncertainty	• Provide proof.
• Minor drawback	• Show big picture.
• Actual obstacle	• Take action.

☐ **Confirm That the Process Is Still Moving Forward.** Resolve the objection and confirm that your prospect feels comfortable moving forward.

Questions you can ask your prospect:
- Has what I said helped address your concern?
- Is everything okay?
- Is everything all right with the solution?
- Are you okay with what we have come up with together?
- Will this solution help out?

Sample Statements to Advance the Process
- Let's move forward together.
- Let's make sure these concerns are addressed.

Avoid Pitfalls

- Don't be afraid of objections. A complaint is actually your friend. This means the customer wants you to succeed, since he has provided a way for you to improve.
- Don't think that because you are talking you are winning a customer over. Some customers internalize their "no" statements and are tuning you out.

Maintenance Check

- Welcome objections and have your customer put them all out on the table.
- Answer the objection(s) clearly, acknowledging what your customer says in mirror language.
- Confirm with the customer that the objection has been resolved so you both can move forward in the Dual Process.

Peaceful Selling Final Thoughts

Now that you have completed your journey into peaceful selling, you can feel confident about setting targets, understanding your prospect's needs, and identifying characteristics of those you can successfully take through the Dual Process.

By knowing where you are in the Dual Process, you can feel at peace about selling your way. We hope you will have patience and let wisdom be your guide.

May the God of hope fill you with all joy and peace as you trust in him, so that you may overflow with hope by the power of the Holy Spirit.

Paul/Saul of Tarsus, Romans, 15:13 (NIV)

About the Authors

Dan Duster is more than a salesperson. He sits on numerous boards, conducts training for personal development and goal achievement, and he still holds one of the largest picnics on the lakefront of Chicago for his high school, college friends, and colleagues. He loves people. One of his favorite hobbies is playing bid whist, where he welcomes any and everyone to challenge him.

Dan has worked for some of the nation's Fortune 100 companies and received the best sales training anyone could ever have. He married his passion for sales with the skills of training and became one of the most decorated salespeople in his area. In 1999, Dan felt the need to formally begin helping people get over their fear of selling.

🐦 DanDuster7
f facebook.com/dan.duster.1
DanDuster.net

Stan Washington, a McDonald's executive turned entrepreneur is founder and president of Honor Services Office, software that helps small businesses grow sales, market businesses, and process invoices easily. He has helped thousands of small businesses achieve sales into the millions. His leadership of operations and technology enabled multi-billion-dollar corporations to increase sales and he is ready to share their tips. Stan also is the coauthor of *Plans to Prosper: Strategies Systems and Tools for Small Business Marketing Success*.

🐦 KunakaNotes
f HonorServicesOffice
in HSO Small Business Innovators
HonorServicesOffice.com

Dan and Stan met at the University of Illinois and have consulted on sales techniques throughout the years. They both saw a need to assist those who are in business to overcome the barrier of selling. The result is this resource.

Other Business Resources

We truly hope you enjoy your new sales process. Here are some other resources you can leverage to help grow your business:

Marketing Growth Tools

Plans to Prosper: Strategies, Systems and Tools for Small Business Marketing Success. Victoria Cook and Stan Washington. Copyright © 2015 ISBN: 978-0-9909831-0-1.

Plans to Prosper: Strategies, Systems and Tools Workbook. Victoria Cook and Stan Washington Copyright © 2015 ISBN: 978-0-9909831-0-1.

Sales Growth Tools

Peaceful Selling: Easy Sales Techniques Workbook. Dan Duster and Stan Washington. Copyright © 2015 ISBN: 978-0-9909831-4-9.

Business Management Software

Honor Services Office is a small business management tool that provides an easy-to-use CRM, an online invoice/bookkeeping system, and an email marketing system.

Visit **http://www.HonorServicesOffice.com** and use promo code: **peacefulselling** to receive your discount.

www.ingramcontent.com/pod-product-compliance
Lightning Source LLC
Chambersburg PA
CBHW070932210326
41520CB00021B/6902